RESURRECTION THEN AND NOW

RESURRECTION
THEN AND NOW

by
JAMES McLEMAN

J. B. LIPPINCOTT COMPANY
Philadelphia and New York
1967

Printed in the United States of America
Library of Congress Catalog Card No.: 67-13304

AUTHOR'S NOTE

I wish to thank Messrs Oliver & Boyd, Ltd. for kind permission to include chapters from my essay *The Birth of the Christian Faith* published by them in 1962. These chapters appear as Part III of the present book.

Biblical quotations are generally from the Revised Standard Version (Nelson, 1952). Quotations from the Apocrypha are from the Revised Version.

CONTENTS

INTRODUCTION

A century ago there was little disposition on the part of Christians to accept any interpretation of the doctrine of resurrection which was not based on a belief in a literal rising from the dead. Today, however, numbers of Christians would admit that they do not believe in bodily resurrection.

The reasons for this development are twofold. One is the changed climate of opinion in which religious thought has to exist in the modern world; the other is the researches of Christians themselves into the origin and validity of their traditional beliefs.

The culture of the present day as expressed in art, literature, politics, etc., is not theo-centric. It is not therefore prone to be inspired by theological considerations or to support theological interpretations of the meaning of life as a matter of preference. Furthermore, a great deal more is known about the basic documents of the faith and the nature of religion in general. The consequence is that it is now impossible to maintain some of the traditional tenets in their time-honoured form.

A man's attitude to religion today is not generally regarded as a matter of life and death with imponderable consequences beyond death. Religious belief is thought of as arising from within the man himself, his spontaneous response to what he finds in experience. He will not allow that it can legitimately be imposed from without. He reserves the right to accept what he feels he needs and let the rest lie.

Rightly or wrongly, he would say that if you can't believe, you can't believe and that's the end of it. "The Church says" or "The Bible says" no longer commands or inspires automatic consent. Beliefs have to prove themselves in face of intelligent inquiry.

It would be a mistake to imagine that this change in the general attitude to religion has come about entirely as a result of pressure from without. It is true that conservative Christians have resented it and some still do. There is no need to illustrate the fact that every advance in science, every victory of knowledge over obscurantism and superstition, has provoked protest on the part of sincere, dogmatic believers. But it is Christian thinkers who have been in the vanguard of investigation into the truth and value of traditional beliefs.

Christian scholars themselves have been the first to realise that a Christianity on the defensive, a Christianity which cannot hold its own in a world of increasing knowledge and improving techniques for discovering truth, is doomed to be superseded. They have been in the front rank in archaeological research, textual criticism, the psychology of religion and other related spheres of research.

Such men do not lament over the fact that the Church and the Scriptures can no longer prescribe beliefs on pain of damnation. They recognise that the word of the Church and of the Scriptures, however valuable, can be only a form of authority but never the seat of authority. To make this plain is a service to truth. To go back on this, to propagate a religion which requires men to isolate their religious thinking from the insights that are common to the everyday life, is to admit that such a religion can have nothing to say to modern man.

In a lecture at Cambridge in 1943, Canon Raven

expressed the point in these words: "To be a Christian or at least to hold official position in the Churches is to accept formulae parts of which can only be explained by being explained away or else to keep secular knowledge and religious knowledge in permanent estrangement. To ask men to live in two such irreconcilable worlds is to imperil the possibility of the wholeness of life which is our need." That the position has changed much since then would be hard to demonstrate.

Continuous re-assessment of the things that have been most surely believed is urgently necessary for the Church of today and among them the matter of resurrection.

No man could repeat today the words of the Apostles' Creed, "I believe ... the resurrection of the body", without being aware of a strain not felt by his counterpart a century ago. The subject is beset by a multitude of ethical, theological and religious misgivings which were hardly conceivable then.

What does believe mean? Has it a specialised meaning in Church? Does body mean body? If, as some say, it means personality, does this mean everything but body? Is it necessary and legitimate to say in this context what you do not mean? If so, why and to what purpose?

Caught in this cross-fire of perplexing questions it is not surprising if some thinking people draw the conclusion that it cannot matter much. If religion is a matter of conundrum and equivocation, then let those who like that sort of thing have it. It would seem to follow that the Church, if it is anxious to influence the thought and life of men today, must come to grips with the difficulties that are patently present in this situation. If the Church does not maintain the intellectual respect of thinking men, it will be resigning itself to becoming a sect and renouncing all claim to be the agent of God's will in the world.

As long ago as 1930, Dr. Edwyn Bevan charitably put the case as it appears to an increasing number of devout and thoughtful people:

"In speaking of the belief in a literal resurrection of the body, the shape and distribution of limbs and organs remaining as they are in normal human bodies now, we are speaking of a belief to which large numbers of Christians certainly and, I think, large numbers of Jews, are still attached. It is a dogma to which the great Roman Church is committed: you may read the very serious discussion of some of the problems it raises in the Catechism of the Council of Trent; how much at the resurrection a man would have of the hair which had been his in life, what would happen in the case of people who, by deformity here, had an excessive number of fingers or toes and so on. A belief which is still held by a large number of people for whose goodness I feel a deep reverence and who are, many of them, quite as qualified as myself to estimate the philosophic implications of any theory, is one which I should be sorry to speak of with anything but respect. Yet it remains true that for many other people today—probably for most educated Christians outside the Roman communion, and most educated Jews—the idea of a literal resurrection of the body has become impossible."*

The following chapters review the idea of resurrection in ancient Judaism and early Christianity and in the history of the Church. Works of immense erudition are available on particular aspects and periods, some of which are quoted and suggested for further reading. But here the attempt is made to give a conspectus of the subject

* *The Hope of a World to Come*, Allen & Unwin, 1930, p. 53.

and to indicate some of the implications which such a historical review enforces on us.

If I may in a sentence anticipate the kind of conclusion the evidence does not preclude, it is that what we have to do with is not an event but a conviction, and that the focus of attention in this matter is not on something which has happened or will happen but on the capabilities of the human soul in relation to its conception of communion with God.

No man can believe in resurrection unless such belief is both available to him and acceptable to him. This is as obvious as that the germ theory of disease could not exist before the invention of the microscope and the acceptance of biogenesis.

Had the prophet Amos, for example, lived in the 1st instead of the 8th century B.C., he would almost certainly have believed in resurrection. As it is, it is as likely that St. Francis believed in space travel. It was not historically possible for his convictions to take this form; the belief was not available to him in the time and circumstances in which he lived.

Again, the Pharisees of Jesus' time were convinced believers in resurrection. But the Sadducees of the same period regarded this tenet as an unwarranted innovation. The belief was available, but to them it was unacceptable; just as the idea of evolution is available but unacceptable to those who hold the verbal inspiration of Genesis.

Whatever more is to be said, therefore, resurrection is both an idea and a conviction. It rises, grows and develops in the context of human thought and has a history; it requires a congenial setting within the consciousness of the individual believer.

About any particular period, what men have believed and why are probably the questions that are most rewarding.

Any worthwhile investigation of the subject of resurrection will require that due weight should be given to both history and experience. Knowledge of the history is not knowledge of the thing itself; conviction regarding the thing itself may be worthless, except to the individual believer, unless it is illuminated by the understanding that comes from insight into its history.

Throughout this study the aim has been to avoid preferring abstract idea to historical embodiment and to refrain from using history to defend specific convictions; neither to rationalise nor to evangelise but to understand.

This is the aim, but it cannot be achieved except in intention. How difficult it is even to keep the intention consistently in mind, let alone to have any assurance of having gone some way in the right direction, only those who have tried will know.

Henry J. Cadbury once said: "It requires real skill and a disciplined historical imagination to appreciate the fundamental difference which exists between situations ancient and modern in which individuals apparently act and think alike." The author is aware of many limitations. If, however, he is able to show what needs to be done and how it might be accomplished, the immediate intention will have been fulfilled.

PART I

THE HISTORICAL SETTING

CHAPTER ONE

IN THE BEGINNING

THE seeds of man's greatest thoughts are buried deep in the unwritten and irrecoverable history of the race. They are the beginnings of his awareness of the conditions and possibilities of human life. Experience brings them more sharply into focus and what we later call original ideas are only the refinements of basic, necessary attitudes to the inescapable circumstances of existence. Our ability to modify these circumstances and to re-direct our notion of what it means to be alive is strictly limited.

The idea of resurrection may be as old as the idea of the rising of the sun if we could trace it to its origin.

Wherever men are able to realise the need and the possibility of making or marking a new start, the idea of resurrection is present in embryo. Even in its highly developed form it is much older than the opening of the Christian era.

The notion of beginning again has a wide natural use in describing what happens in the everyday experience of men. The repetitious content of life makes it necessary to have some category which will indicate the simple fact that the mind is aware of both sameness and newness in consecutive experience. This is one of the primary conditions of learning. Without it men could not have a history.

When we observe the agricultural year, for instance, it is as a unit which repeats or at least resembles itself again and again. But we have previously observed the recurring sequence of day and night. We have repeated in time and in our own experience many duties and journeys. We are familiar with beginnings and endings and new beginnings.

To this extent, therefore, it may be said that the general idea of resurrection is native to man from an early stage in his history. It is a means or method of conceiving and expressing an indigenous aspect of his experience. It is given as one of the conditions of his life as a thinking being.

But along with this (and equally necessary to the ability to learn), is the possibility of applying a conception in thought to a different but analogous situation. If we link the idea of beginning again with the idea of likeness —not merely the thought that what begins anew is generically like what preceded it, but that one new beginning is like another—we have the possibility of a metaphorical use of the idea of resurrection.

An incident or fact can be described in terms of a metaphor derived from observing something different in every respect except one. We may speak, for instance, of a burning passion, a cloud of suspicion, a storm of controversy and be quite aware that the fact we are describing is different from the fact of the metaphor except in one essential respect.

Now the idea of resurrection is by its nature irresistible for use in this metaphorical fashion. It is distinct, dramatic and readily applicable to a variety of situations. It is appropriate to some of our most intense emotions such as surprise, wonder, exultation.

Our life is enclosed in circumstances that are fittingly described as being like life from the dead. And such hyperbole will pass without comment. Escape, rescue, hope, good fortune, recovery of health are all capable of being expressed metaphorically as "new life" and "rising from the dead". They are like in the sense of constituting a new beginning. A man may "come back" from illness and be as one "returned from the dead". Good news may make a "new man" of him.

In our case we have inherited the metaphor. But let us turn to the situation where it is only being created with all the force of originality. We are fortunate in having such a precise instance.

In 597 B.C. Nebuchadnezzar overthrew the small Hebrew state and carried numerous Jews into exile in Babylon. Eleven years later it was found necessary to capture and lay waste Jerusalem itself. It seemed the end of Hebrew history.

Among the exiles was the prophet Ezekiel. His writings contain forecasts of the restoration of the Jewish people and the reconstitution of the Jewish state.

The most remarkable of those prophecies from our point of view is in chapter 37 in which he "sees" a vision of a valley of dry bones. It is a powerful and realistic profession of faith in the resurgence of Israel's national life based on vividly described physical resurrection. The dry bones are made to live.

It is important to note that the prophet is not describing the future in terms of something he has seen in the past. He is using the notion of physical resurrection, itself derived from the application to man's existence of the general conception of beginning again, to reinforce his forecast of improvement in his nation's fortunes.

The psychology of prophecy is a difficult matter with which we are not concerned. We only note the expression which the prophet gives to his prophetic insight as a simple fact which raises questions that have a bearing on our subject.

Is the application of the idea of resurrection to man's existence a natural development and extension of metaphor? Or is there a factual limit beyond which the metaphorical conception of resurrection does not extend?

The sun rises; the nation can rise; news may be as life from the dead. But that a dead man may live again does not seem to be a member of the series. At least, it has not seemed to be so in the estimation of most men. Jastrow in his *Religion of Babylon and Assyria* (1898), p. 577, says, "the suffering individual stricken with disease could be awakened to new life. It is this 'restoration' which lies in the power of the gods, but once a man has been carried off to Aralu, no god can bring him back to earth."

For all the particularity of Ezekiel's description of bones becoming living men again, no scholar would assert that Ezekiel believed in the physical resurrection of the body after death. He is not declaring that men rise from the dead: he is insisting that the nation will prosper. The metaphor is known to be a metaphor—a startling one to perform a startling duty.

Ezekiel is saying that Israel appears to be finished, but this is not so. She will continue to exist as a nation— even if this seems as unbelievable and as miraculous as that dead men will get up and walk!

But Ezekiel never saw dead men rise; nor did he expect to. "Ezekiel's vision of the Valley of Dry Bones is a metaphor, describing the restoration of the Jewish people, and not a promise of actual and individual resurrection."*

But if we turn the pages of history we do come on a period when it was undoubtedly believed that in particular circumstances men, at least certain men, would literally be resurrected. They spoke of the resurrection of the

* H. Wheeler Robinson, *The Religious Ideas of the Old Testament*, p. 97 n.

dead and they meant quite unequivocally the resurrection of the dead.

How, when and why did this transition beyond what may be the normal limit of metaphor in the use of this idea take place? Under what circumstances did men find it possible to use resurrection as applied to human beings no longer as a metaphor but as a forecast of fact?

Sometime between the age of Ezekiel and the beginnings of Christianity the resurrection of the dead had become a commonplace of belief.

This means that belief in resurrection was not a natural tenet among the Hebrews during the major part of their pre-Christian history. The kingdoms of Israel and Judah have come and gone, the great prophets have made their amazing contribution to Hebrew theology, and still there is no doctrine of resurrection. In the whole of the Old Testament, scholars will allow only two passages as expressing the idea in literal description of what may happen to (certain) men after death.

These two passages are Isaiah 26:19 and Daniel 12:2. Not all would agree that the former is a case in point and it is generally recognised that both belong to the latest period represented in the Old Testament Canon. The second cannot be dated earlier than the middle of the 2nd century B.C.

But beyond this period there is a great change. Comparing the Judaism of the year 350 B.C. with that of A.D. 50, C. G. Montefiore says, "The fundamental difference would be that in 350 B.C. the average Jew believed that, so far as any bliss or happiness was concerned (whether lower or higher), death was the end; whereas in A.D. 50 he believed that, for the righteous at any rate, the higher happiness would actually not be experienced till beyond the grave. The importance of the conception of a future life and of the resurrection of the dead in Judaism can hardly be over-estimated. Gunkel observes rightly that these ideas materially changed the entire religion; they are so epoch-making that they divide the whole religious history of Israel into two sections—before and after them."

This, of course, is not equivalent to saying there was no belief in a future life within the Old Testament period. There never was such a situation. The quality of such after-life was matter of speculation then as now. But of the fact that belief in its existence was general, evidence is to be found throughout. The one exception of note is some verses in Ecclesiastes where a sophisticated philosopher of the time finds he cannot rise above scepticism or very radical agnosticism. "A living dog is better than a dead lion. The living know they shall die: but the dead know not anything" (Eccl. 9:4, 5 (A.V.)).

Man appears to be incapable of conceiving of his own personal non-existence. He can conceive of the end of life as he knows it, but not of the end of "himself". Nevertheless, the onlooker is impressed by the terminal aspect of death: he has to exercise faith and hope beyond it almost by an act of will. In some way the end must not be the end only. What kind of continuity can be envisaged?

That throughout the Old Testament period this continuity or after-life is not thought of as the reconstitution of man on the other side of death is not to be wondered at. Here Israel was at one with mankind. What is remarkable is that at a particular period in her history she is found to be in possession of a belief in resurrection from the dead and to stand alone in this—except for the followers of Zarathustra.

In tracing the history of the idea of progress, John Baillie has occasion to note the fact that Israel and Zoroastrianism are unique in their conviction that history has a goal.

"Only twice in the history of thought," he says, "has the idea arisen that history might be tracing another pattern than the circular one, and in both these cases it was the same general pattern that was proposed, namely, that of a non-recurrent movement towards the ultimate triumph of good. This is the conception which unites the religion of the Magi with that of the Hebrews and which differentiates them from all other religions and philosophies save those which have drawn some degree of inspiration from them—Mithraism from the one, Christianity and Islam and Western thought in general from the other."*

It is surely significant that the beginning of the idea of progress is discovered in religions which are essentially prophetic and that belief in resurrection takes its rise in these precise circumstances.

But we must return to this later. Meantime we consider the forms which belief about what happens after death have taken, the prolegomena to Christian and Western thought on the subject.

* *The Belief in Progress*, Oxford, 1950, pp. 57, 58.

CHAPTER TWO

SURVIVAL, IMMORTALITY AND RESURRECTION

It is not only religious man but man himself, whatever his attitude to religion, who is compelled to think of what the meaning of death is, and what if anything lies beyond it. What he thinks will depend on his ability to interpret the needs and possibilities of the general setting of his life in his particular age.

The range of possible thought on a subject like this is vast. But the constriction of custom and tradition, repressive in primitive cultures and still considerable even in more developed societies, sets limits to the possible patterns of thought and behaviour. In fact the alternatives are reduced to a very few which are repeated and refined throughout the general course of human history.

Because the idea of resurrection comes to its full development in Jewish thought and is affected by cognate ideas of immortality derived from Greek speculation, it is necessary for us to distinguish between early Hebrew notions of the after-life, immortality and resurrection and to note the distinctiveness of the last named.

In the Old Testament period we find nothing remarkable in the references to the after-life. It is thought of on analogy with what happens in life, a bloodless counterpart to our present existence to which no one can look forward with other emotions than resignation, regret or foreboding. Death is not the end, but what is beyond is not to be compared with life and certainly not to be longed for.

"The dead are supposed to go on existing in some sense or other, even by the early thought of Israel. But it is an existence which has no attraction for the Israelite, and falls outside the sphere of his proper religion. It is not his soul that survives at all; the dead are called 'shades' (*rephaim*) not 'souls', in the Old Testament. The (subterranean) place of their abiding is called Sheol, and in many particulars is like the Greek Hades. Sheol seems to be an outgrowth of the family grave, probably under the influence of Babylonian ideas."[*]

The rule of Yahweh, Israel's God, does not extend beyond life. To die is to go to the land of the shadow of death in dark and joyless exile. A vivid description of Sheol occurs in Isaiah 14:9–11 and another in Ezekiel 32:18 f.

This is a conception which is characteristic of men in a society in an unreflective and custom-ridden stage of development. Life is absorbed in the business of daily living. The individual is important only as a member of a tribe and the god "knew and cared for the individual only as a member of the community".[†]

In such a community death is the other man's death, of significance to the community which it depletes but not capable of initiating independent hopes, a cul-de-sac as far as thought and inspiration are concerned, beyond which no progress was possible.

The idea of immortality of the soul, on the other hand, arises in a society where reflection is initiated by those who are no longer completely enfolded in the life of a community with a "defective sense of individuality". It is a conception which is bound together with a man's notion of his own being and the nature of his "soul".

[*] H. Wheeler Robinson, *Religious Ideas of the Old Testament*, p. 92.
[†] Robertson Smith, *The Religion of the Semites*, p. 259.

It is among the Greeks that we find its highest development.

Orphic brotherhoods taught the pre-existence of the soul and recognised in consequence an inherent immortality. Man is akin to the divine. The body is a tomb from which death will liberate the soul to everlasting joy.

"Orphism insisted on a radical distinction of the soul as spiritual and the body as earthly. In terrestrial life the soul is imprisoned in the body. The true significance of history is to be found in the soul gaining its emancipation from the physical. . . . For the Orphics there was a change of focus of vision from this world to a spiritual world beyond, and with this an advocacy of an asceticism alien to the Greek attitude of moderation in a harmonious psychophysical life."*

In Plato this strain of thought is refined into an alluring and lofty philosophy which evokes a distinctive attitude to life.

C. C. J. Webb in his *History of Philosophy* (p. 33) indicates a point of transition from ecstatic religious surmise to the sublime serenity of the Platonic doctrine. Speaking of the Pythagorean contribution to Greek thought he says: "On the one hand, it brought into new prominence certain superstitious beliefs and practices of primitive, not to say savage, origin; on the other hand it deepened the sense of individual dignity and responsibility by its doctrine of the immortality and transmigration of souls".

There is here an immense advance on the "underworld" conception of life after death. The primitive conception involves a communal abode of the dead such as Hades or Sheol where they "sleep with their fathers", for man has only communal significance. The reflective notion takes account of the essential worthwhileness of man and leads

* Alban G. Widgery, *Interpretations of History*, 1961, p. 68.

to a doctrine of personal and to that extent individual immortality.

But in the third conception, that of resurrection, it is not the common fate of mankind or the individual worth of man that is formative. The primary factor here is what is believed about God and what this belief allows to be possible as an answer to the question, "After death, what?" This cannot arise except where religion is a commanding interest beyond the primitive level and not merely one of many.

The signal instance is, of course, the Hebrew tradition in the period after the Exile, to which we must shortly give close attention. But it would appear that phases of Egyptian and Persian history would furnish other though less pronounced examples. When thought about the other side of death comes to its climax within such a tradition, it tends to arrive at or point towards a form of resurrection.

In Egypt, for instance, "a death and resurrection motive" was introduced into the cultus in the Osiris myth and after *c.* 1400 B.C. the hoped-for blessings were not confined to the royal house.* The Book of the Dead gives magical formulae whereby the dead, if they so desire, may resume their former bodies.

Mummification aimed at making the body tissues imperishable and preserving the likeness of the deceased so that it can "continue its former life in its fulness in the delectable fields of Aalu watered by the heavenly Nile, or in the celestial realms of Re where the sun never sets".

Precise theory here may be out of our reach, may indeed be impossible because never clearly conceived. There is some evidence that the body may have been

* See e.g. E. O. James, *The Social Function of Religion*, pp. 80 ff.

regarded as the seed of whatever existence was considered possible beyond the grave.

For our purpose all that is important is that here, under a deeply religious aegis, the body is conceived as being necessarily included in whatever may come after death. This appears to be the only sufficient reason for the elaborate attempts to prevent it from becoming indistinguishable from the dust of the earth. This is the direction that thought can take in a given tradition where religion is consciously dominant. Religion tends to demand in such an instance a fuller and more concrete form of hereafter than the irreparable sundering of a body–soul relationship is capable of providing. In short, it requires resurrection rather than immortality.

How far this is due to lack of capacity for a more abstract type of thought is a nice point. But it is at least arguable that where pressure towards the idea of resurrection appears, it is largely the result of a religious need for an enriched conception of what awaits the pious on the other side of death. God will reward His servant by restoring his own life with interest. This is what cannot be said of the primitive or reflective conceptions. The primitive hereafter is only a shadow of the present; the reflective hereafter is not the same as the present; the religious is required to be the same at its best.

The dating of the documents on which we depend for our knowledge of Zoroastrianism and Iranian beliefs about life after death is still matter for dispute. The question is of great importance in any attempt to assess the influence of Persian thought on other cultures. But it is admitted that here we have a tradition which is the result of vigorous religious interest and in this tradition thought of "after death" culminates in a conception of resurrection.

The eschatology of Zoroastrianism is highly developed and is of absorbing interest when compared with Judaic and Christian doctrines of the last things or the end of the world. All that we note at the moment is what is taught regarding the mode of life in the "age to come". When evil is banished in the golden age of Ahura, all men will be resurrected bodily at the appearance of the Divine Deliverer (Saoshyant) to undergo trial by ordeal which will decide their eternal destiny.

The "last turning point in creation" is described in the Gathas. When the Saoshyant comes the world will be engulfed in a flood of molten metal. The wicked will be consumed but the righteous will survive unscathed and the kingdom of Ahura Mazdah will then be set up. Then "they that get them good name shall be partakers in the promised reward in the fair abode of Good Thought, of Mazdah, and of Right" (Ys. XXX, 10).

Zoroaster thought of himself as commissioned to purify religion (Ys. XLIV, 9) and it has even been said that "no religion has so clearly grasped the ideas of guilt and of merit" (Geldner). Here we have an even more direct and conclusive instance of the thrust of religion in the direction of a distinctive doctrine of life after death. Here the doctrine is unsophisticated and stands out starkly against a plain background like a strong, crude piece of sculpture by an unschooled but inspired hand.

Zoroastrianism appears to be the creation of prophetic thinking. This raises the question, "When and how does a religion reach the point of dominance which endows it with creative freedom to draw such firm conclusions about the ultimate fate of its devotees?" This kind of historical and critical question is extremely important in its own place.

What we have been trying to maintain so far is simply

that it is religion which attains to the particular concept which we recognise as the idea of human resurrection, religion at a dominant stage in which the idea of God is commanding to the extent of supporting a belief in God's power and purpose to raise the dead.

That religion in some of its phases has not produced this idea is due either to the fact that it has not yet attained the self-consciousness to be concerned about the destiny of the individual, or to the fact that it has become sufficiently sophisticated to have found its expression of concern for the destiny of the individual in a doctrine of the reflective type which leads to some variety of belief in the immortality of the soul.

This thesis can be worked out particularly in regard to post-exilic Judaism. Here religion reached a position of priority and an ethical intensity which is perhaps unique in history.

Religion after the Exile was recognised to be the most intimate, personal and predominant concern of the individual Israelite. It is in this content that the idea of resurrection comes to its clearest and most intense expression.

It should therefore be possible to maintain that where religious faith is both vital and personal and has free course to answer the question as to what is beyond death out of its own essence, without the aid of philosophical speculation, it leads directly to a doctrine of resurrection. Religion which is theological rather than metaphysical will postulate resurrection rather than immortality.

CHAPTER THREE

TIDES OF THOUGHT

ANYONE who is familiar with the literature of what is known as the inter-Testamental period will not need to be convinced that this is the key period for the study of our subject. Here the idea of resurrection reached its ultimate and exercised its maximum influence as a commanding conception in history among the Jews of that age.

Two points should be made clear. The first is that this does not involve the thesis that the idea of resurrection developed along a precise line and issued in one paramount doctrine. This is patently not so. There is here no systematic doctrine of resurrection, just as there is no systematic doctrine of eschatology as a whole. The conception of orthodoxy in doctrine is yet to be born. Judaism's orthodoxy is an orthodoxy of life and behaviour. What we have is an efflorescence of the resurrection idea of remarkable range and scope which makes this period in relation to our subject analogous to the renaissance in relation to European culture.

The second point is that if our assessment of this period is justified, we must look backward for some of the root ideas which were the stuff of inter-Testamental-thought, as well as forward to the fruit in New Testament doctrine. Our plan is therefore presented to us in outline. We must consider the beginnings of the thought of resurrection in so far as we can uncover them. We must take a closer look at the crucial period itself and the factors responsible for its particular ethos. We must examine the bearing of all this upon the first age of Christian history in the New Testament literature.

We turn in this chapter to the beginnings of the idea of resurrection, the idea which came to such rampant expression between 200 B.C. and A.D. 100. This is a notoriously difficult subject and it is immensely complicated by a psychological disability to which many investigators are prone.

Something should be said here on this psychological factor first of all. A man who is investigating the particular past with which he is anxious to identify himself is apt to give himself and his chosen ally the benefit of the doubt, if there is any doubt. Books of history and religion abound with examples. Many writers are urgently concerned with substantiating the purity of their genealogy in racial, national, religious or ideological terms. Worthiness in some respect or other makes the issue a point of honour.

This natural vested interest is not necessarily consciously pursued. It is, nevertheless, often potent and vicious. It would seem that only those who are simply glad to be alive and believe in God are unconcerned that they—and all men—are mongrels in most respects.

Christian writers are apparently content that the roots of their faith are to be found in Judaism, albeit Judaism as interpreted by themselves. But let anyone try to suggest that either Judaism or Christianity is indebted in the least degree to Egypt, Babylonia, Persia or Greece for any of the significant forms of thought which they now regard as distinctively their own, and there are some who will raise a hurricane of outraged protest.

But it is surely not an iniquitous idea that the seeds of some plants that grew in the garden of Judaism and were later transplanted to the ampler garden of Christianity were carried over the wall in the first place from other areas of religious genius. It is too late in the day to try to confine religious genius within strictly racial or conventional religious boundaries.

We have already noticed that only two brief passages which refer definitely to the resurrection of the body, and those very late, are to be found in the Old Testament. It can be stated quite definitely that the idea of resurrection as a prerogative of religious men is absent from the literature of Israel belonging to pre-exilic and early post-exilic times. This is remarkable for two reasons.

The first is that it amounts to saying that the Israelites, a people of unique religious genius whose history even before the exile presented them with excruciating situations in which a doctrine of resurrection would have been immensely valuable psychologically, did not come to the point of excogitating or intuiting such a doctrine to meet its spiritual need. For instance, the agonies of doubt in Job and some of the Psalms, the impassioned and almost shameless pleading for assurance, for existential security, derive their depth in part from the finality of death and the shuddering anticipation of the darkness and aridity of Sheol. And this literature is largely early post-exilic.

The second thing is that the belief in resurrection in Judaism, like many other kindred beliefs of an eschatological character, arises after the period of the Dispersion. It comes into its own in the exigencies of the church-state of post-exilic Judaism. The constraints of history allowed no freedom for development of either ecclesiastical or political ambitions. What was left was the valour of being prepared to die if need be for the Torah (symbol of Israel's veiled religious and national greatness), which was so starkly incarnated in the Maccabean Revolt of 168 B.C.

This resistance was maintained with such passion and

purpose as almost defied what might be regarded as the inevitabilities or probabilities of the historical situation. The restoration of the kingdom was a *tour de force* which is probably unparalleled in history. This was the forcing house which brought out the flourish of apocalyptic literature that characterised the period.

We note the difference in reaction to historical pressure as between pre-exilic and post-exilic times. Pre-exilic Hebrews submitted, though not gracefully, to the bludgeoning of world powers and hoped for better days. Post-exilic Judaism refused to submit and continued to hope.

Thus when the northern kingdom was confronted with the threat of oppression (which ended in the obliteration of the northern kingdom of Israel in 722 B.C.), Amos declared at the royal sanctuary that this encroachment was the work and will of Yahweh. "The high places of Isaac shall be desolate, and the sanctuaries of Israel shall be laid waste: and I will rise against the house of Jeroboam with the sword" (Amos 7:7 ff.).

Hosea's judgment on the political situation of the time reflected the same lack of confidence in Israel's righteousness; she has not the necessary morale to make a stand against the oppressor. Yahweh is not on the nation's side in this matter of conflict between Israel and the oppressor. "They have set up kings (six in rapid succession), but not by me; they have made princes and I knew it not."*

It is true that Isaiah for a time gives support to the spirit of resistance in the southern kingdom of Judah. "What then shall one answer the messengers of the nation? That Yahweh hath founded Zion and in her shall the afflicted of his people take refuge" (Isaiah 14:32). But this is resignation ("quietness and confidence") rather than defiance.

* Hosea 8:4, trans. H. Wheeler Robinson.

When the real crisis arrived Jeremiah condemned the plot among smaller, satellite states against Babylon. The yoke of Babylon rested on the shoulders of the nations by Yahweh's will and it could not be broken (see Jeremiah, chaps. 27 and 28). The hope of the future was in the exiles, i.e. those who submitted to Yahweh's destruction of present nationality at the hands of the heathen (chap. 29).

Post-exilic Judaism in the 2nd century was confronted with a similar political situation. Antiochus IV wielded the might that formerly belonged to Assyria and Babylon and the Jewish state was equally frail. But the reaction was quite different—resistance even unto death.

The speech of Judas in 1 Maccabees 3 expresses the temper of the times. "It is an easy thing for many to be shut up in the hands of a few; and with heaven it is all one, to save by many or by few: for victory in battle standeth not in the multitude of a host; but strength is from heaven. They come to us in fulness of insolence and lawlessness, to destroy us and our wives and our children for to spoil us: but we fight for our lives and our laws. And he himself will discomfit them before our face: but as for you, be ye not afraid of them."

To account for this change of temper we have to allow for the manifold changes in outlook and experience that had taken place during the Exile and in the period from the Return onwards. But it seems to be true that one reason why Judaism, which had discovered deep distinctive convictions, now refused to submit and continued to hope with such fanatical devotion, was the fact that death now meant glory because of belief in resurrection.

The hammer blows of history did not forge belief in resurrection in pre-exilic days. Nor did they forge it in the later period, though they gave it form and content sufficient for the day. The intervening period of Dispersion and contact with other cultures is the crucial factor in tracing the rise and growth of resurrection belief in Israel.

Briefly, the Exile was the university of Judaism. The boy from the provinces is brought to the metropolis. He looks out on the world and history with new eyes. The skyline of that broad land of Babylonia was broken not by the mountains from which Yahweh uttered His voice, but by colossal buildings proclaiming the might and genius of an imperium absolute and arrogant whose God was not the Lord. The captive Jews, and their descendants who never returned to the land of their fathers, gazed on temples, palaces, pleasure gardens and all the lavish evidence of wealth and skill. They thought new thoughts on the meaning of power and culture. To see and learn and not to be changed, this is impossible. Their prophets warned, upbraided and denounced because the lure of heathen thoughts and ways was not negligible.

In the light of this experience the Jews re-wrote their own history and transposed their prophecy into a different key. Apocalyptic is the prophecy of the post-exilic era.

Some Jews returned to broken Jerusalem but the Dispersion continued. With the passage of time Jewish settlements were to be found all over the empire.

The Jews of the Dispersion formed "a world-wide organisation of a nation and a religion, permeating an immense empire and extending far beyond its frontiers. The Jews outside Palestine were a people practically ignored by Greek and Roman antiquity, scarcely heeded in their classical literature. If noticed at all they were scoffed at as beggars or credulous imposters, but nevertheless they had filled the world, and their settlements formed a series of posts along the great highways of trade and empire from the Persian Gulf to the Atlantic."*

* Jackson and Lake, *The Beginnings of Christianity*, Vol. 1, p. 168.

But were not these Israelites exclusive, fanatical for the ancient religion of Israel, incapable of corruption by the thoughts and habits of the heathen? To some extent, no doubt. But it is a mistake to project the isolationism of later Judaism into the earlier centuries.

Jews of the Dispersion were not impervious to the intellectual and theological climate around them. Pre-exilic Hebrews had not been as immune to the attractions of false gods and idolatrous practices as later editors of the sacred literature would have wished. Even the pre-exilic prophets have defection as a main theme. Then they were in their own land but now enfolded in alien culture.

When we enter the period of Greek domination following the conquests of Alexander the Great the merging of different traditions is commonplace. "The religions of the east and west flowed into one another; it was an age during which beliefs, speculations, superstitions and the like, of a very varied character, impregnated the mental atmosphere of the peoples of the world; ancient cults and rites of a crude and debasing nature which, one might suppose, had disappeared altogether, came to the fore once more; and what fascinated the bulk of the peoples was not likely to leave the Jews untouched."*

Even as early as Ezekiel and 2 Isaiah the use of pagan mythology is evident. If, as is the case, the eschatology which spread from Persia and the eschatology of Judaism have much in common, the natural explanation is syncretism. Some Jewish writers would claim that Judaism gave all that is of value to Iranian eschatology and accepted nothing of consequence. But exclusiveness means inability to give as well as inability to receive. That ideas whose origin is to be found in Iranian

* Oesterley and Robinson, *History of Israel*, Vol. 2, p. 306.

religious traditions surviving in the areas of the Dispersion were absorbed into the general stream of Judaism admits of no doubt. A glance at the differences between early Hebrew and post-exilic eschatology shows that the developments and additions are precisely in the direction of Iranian eschatology. Some are quite incompatible with pre-exilic Hebrew notions.

There is a new world-and-time-awareness which is characteristic of Iranian cosmology. World history is the arena of a contest above the conflict of warring states and is leading to a new era, not simply a time of greater national prosperity. This will be ushered in by catastrophe and conflagration. The righteous will enjoy the new age, even if they have died, for they will be raised and justified.

It might be as well to quote authoritative opinion on this matter. Oesterley and Robinson make this cautious but categorical statement in their *Hebrew Religion* (revised and enlarged edition): "The question as to how far the religion of the Jews was influenced by that of Persia is a very controversial one: some scholars deny any Persian influence, others see a good deal of it. Both extreme positions are probably exaggerated. In one direction it is quite impossible not to see that strong Persian influences have been at work, viz. in the domain of Eschatology and Apocalyptic" (p. 312).

The particular matters in which indebtedness can be detected are listed as follows: (1) a Dualism which is responsible for a conflict between opposing supernatural powers for possession of the world and mankind, (2) Division of time into eras or world-epochs, (3) Judgment and the destruction of the world by fire, (4) the Resurrection of the dead.

The authors point out that only in Iranian eschatology and Jewish apocalyptic are resurrection and judgment connected with world conflagration,* they note his observation that in Jewish eschatology we have both resurrection and judgment at the last day and, alongside, retribution on the individual immediately after death and before resurrection, and that this occurs nowhere else but in Iranian eschatology. The authors continue: "Those two facts mentioned should be sufficient to prove the indebtedness of Jewish Apocalyptists to Persia."†

These are significant additions to pre-exilic eschatology. They are due not to discovery, revelation or excogitation, but to appropriation from a tradition which goes back to Zoroastrianism as its originating source. And these are some of the key ideas of the inter-Testamental period and the New Testament eschatological teaching.

The apocalyptic writers are largely concerned with exploiting these major themes within the context of their own religious tradition in the interest of a people now in the toils of a historical situation which can issue in nothing but national frustration.

During the period, ideas whose origin is Greek rather than eastern will also come within the same area of mental and spiritual travail. They create their own stress as they simultaneously attract and repel the interest of Judaism. This is why the period 200 B.C. to A.D. 100 is a cauldron of controversy.

* Referring to Bousset's *Die Religion des Judentums*, 1926, pp. 511 ff.
† *Op. cit.*, p. 394.

CHAPTER FOUR

THE CRUCIAL PERIOD

WE should reflect that if a new thought cannot be traced in the writers of a particular age, it is certain not to have been prevalent and effective among the ordinary people of the time. We can therefore say that, at least to the middle of the 3rd century B.C., there was no general belief among the Jews that men would be raised from the grave after completing life on earth. The abode of the dead was Sheol from which there was no return.

How then does it happen that when we open the New Testament we are reading a series of documents which could not have been conceived apart from a vivid general belief in resurrection? What had happened between the Testaments?

In some editions of the Bible the Old Testament is separated from the New by one blank leaf. This can be symbolical. But if so, it does not mean that there is nothing to know or nothing we need to know in the period between the end of the Old Testament and the beginning of the New. It means that many people have assumed that a knowledge of whatever took place in that interval is of no consequence—a very profound mistake.

There is no mystery about this inter-Testamental period. The history and thought of the time are available on the same terms as apply to other periods. The literature of the era is known as the Apocrypha and the Pseudepigrapha of the Old Testament and has been readily

available in translation and with commentaries for the
past 50 years.*

Apart from the work of continental scholars, two British
scholars in particular deserve gratitude for their classic
and authoritative researches in this field—R. H. Charles
and W. O. E. Oesterley.

In 1913 Charles, who had already drawn attention to
many of the inter-Testamental works, edited a comprehensive edition in English with introductions and notes
which is still indispensable—*The Apocrypha and Pseudepigrapha of the Old Testament* (2 Vols.). The following
year he issued an outline of the salient ideas of the period
entitled *Religious Development between the Old and New
Testaments*. In it he maintained that "we are now in a
position to prove that these two centuries were in many
respects centuries of greater spiritual progress than any
two that had preceded them in Israel".

In 1914 also came Oesterley's *The Books of the Apocrypha* with the object, as he says, "of pressing home the
importance of one department of the subject". The first
part deals with the life and thought of the period and the
second provides introductions and comments on the
various books. He followed this in 1935 with *An Introduction to the Apocrypha*. More recent books on aspects of
this subject include *The Relevance of Apocalyptic* (1944), by
H. H. Rowley, *The Apocryphal Literature: A brief Introduction* (1945), by C. C. Torrey, *A History of New
Testament Times with an Introduction to the Apocrypha*
(1949), by R. H. Pfeiffer, and *Between the Testaments*
(1960), by D. S. Russell.

Unfortunately the works themselves, and books on

* For a brief history of the fate of those books through the centuries see
two articles by R. H. Pfeiffer in *The Interpreter's Bible*, Vol. 1 (New
York, 1952).

them, tend to be regarded as options for those who may have the leisure to pursue a specialised interest, rather like curiosities of religious literature.

There are two main reasons why it is still necessary today to insist on the importance of this period. One is the increase of specialisation and the other is the fact that transmission of new knowledge from the expert to the place where it becomes effective (i.e. in the thinking of the ordinary Christian about his faith) is still slow.

In common with other subjects, Biblical and theological studies in the past 150 years have exploded into a host of new and specialised departments. The day of the polymath is over. A man takes a lifetime to master his own particular (more and more restricted) branch of study.

While the scholar may keep his eyes open for any special developments in cognate departments (cf. the repercussions caused by the discovery of the Dead Sea Scrolls), it is less easy to embody the findings of others into his own thinking in such a way as to comprehend their full import.

So it happens that even today and even in the case of some whose interest runs close to those which are raised by a study of inter-Testamental literature, it is doubtful if sufficient allowance is made for the adjustments of thought made necessary by the knowledge we now have of what took place between the Testaments.

When we take the next step and consider what is likely to be true at the level of ordinary teaching of religion, e.g. in the ministry of the Church in general, there is even less likelihood of any modification to the thought of the time. Most clergy are aware of the period and have been introduced to it during their training. But it has made no impact comparable, for instance, to that of the work of contemporary continental and American theologians and their popularisers, particularly as the trend has been away from historical and critical investigation and towards neo-dogmatic attitudes.

When we go still further and ask what difference these studies have made to the ordinary Christian's understanding of his faith, the answer is infinitesimal. He is fortunate to have heard of the period. Many are content to think that this is how it ought to be because they fail to see any virtue in faith and knowledge walking hand in hand.

But it is puerile to behave in the manner of the Muslim who ordered the burning of books on the ground that if they contradicted the Koran they were heretical, if they did not they were superfluous. If the books of the inter-Testamental period add nothing to the conviction about resurrection to be found in the New Testament, however much they increase our knowledge of the development of the idea of resurrection (to say nothing of subjects like the kingdom of God, Messiah and the last judgment), it is reckoned a waste of time to study them. Surely this is a concession to wilful ignorance.

The justification for the study of the Old Testament as far as Christianity is concerned is that it throws light on the New in which it is taken for granted. If now it could be shown that on this important matter which is fundamental to the New Testament, namely resurrection, the inter-Testamental thought is more important than the whole of the Old Testament corpus, one might expect a change of attitude.

But today there seems to exist a dogmatic need on the part of some theologians to disown every hypothesis which would seem to modify the uniqueness of the New Testament in the slightest degree. The suggestion that it is possible to retrace continuity and development into a non-canonical era in any respect which is important for Christian theology is still difficult to entertain. Popular expositions of Christianity amply confirm this thesis and in religious studies the gap between the specialist and the ordinary man seems to be as wide and unbridgeable as in any of the sciences.

The study of this era is beset by one particular danger. It is that of becoming so immersed in interesting and confusing details that one is satisfied with the mere attempt to place in order the events and ideas of the period and neglects to consider their impact on the living context of New Testament thought and thence on the development of Christian tradition.

Many books that should take account of this are simply content to give résumés of the history and outlines of the literature as if all this belonged to a compartment of life in parenthesis. It is as if the author were afraid to cross an imaginary boundary between late Jewish literature and the New Testament, as if there were two worlds semi-detached.

But no such boundary exists. The arbitrary selection of a number of documents to be labelled "The New Testament", unique as they are in certain respects, does not *eo ipso* isolate and insulate them from current life and thought. Whence did Paul, for instance, draw his thoughts about resurrection in 1 Corinthians? Whence did Jesus derive His conception of the last judgment? Unless we are prepared to argue that these were received by direct revelation, it is obvious that the inter-Testamental literature is of considerable importance.

It is in the light of this kind of significance that it should be studied—not as fossilised lore, but as the hidden years of many New Testament concepts, the embryo of what stands fully grown in the New Testament period.

It is roughly the last two centuries B.C. and the 1st century A.D. that concern us. After the death of Alexander the Great, his Ptolemaic (Egypt) successors controlled Palestine from 312 to 198 B.C. when the overlordship passed to his Seleucid (Syrian) successors. Under the inspiration of the Maccabean family, the Jews revolted against the most tyrannical of them, Antiochus IV (Epiphanes), in 168. The story from 175 to 135 is recorded in 1 Maccabees, written about the end of the century.

The revolt was successful. The Maccabees succeeded by the Hasmonaeans became the native nominal rulers of a liberated land till Pompey's intervention in 63 B.C. when the country was brought under Roman dominance. The only significant ruler from then till the appointment of Roman Procurators was the alien Herod the Great (37 B.C.–A.D. 4) and the next historic event is the Jewish War and the fall of Jerusalem in A.D. 70.

Thus the only period of quasi-independence during this era (and that a very precarious one) was the result of the Maccabean Revolt. This interval lasted from 142 to 63 B.C. and was a bitter disappointment. The whole age is one of frustration and humiliation from a political point of view. Grim reality made ashes of all but bright hopes.

But if, perhaps because, politically, the Jews were overwhelmed and the hope of a resurgence of the kingdom was blasted, religiously and theologically they made this a creative era. Vigorous thinking brought to prominence hopes that were beyond the touch of Greek or Roman overlords. These hopes were centred on a God who was believed to be able to recreate the world if He so designed, and to set Israel again in her rightful place as His people.

The characteristic of these hopes is their extravagance and profusion. They arose from national and individual piety and were expressed in the language of devotion. Those who led the thought of the time projected their life and the life of the nation into what they believed to be an inevitable age of bouleversement.

In that day it would be woe to the victors and unprecedented triumph to the downtrodden. The kingdom of God would transpose the present subjection of God's people into glorious dominion. All roles would be reversed. Israel, oppressed and despised, would be raised to the heights of blessedness. Her enemies, now proud and victorious, would be plunged into misery and damnation.

Denunciation of the godless and prophecies of ineffable blessing for the righteous abound. Thus in Enoch 92:7 "And when sin and unrighteousness and blasphemy and violence in all kinds of deeds increase and apostasy and transgression and uncleanness abound, then shall a great chastisement of heaven come upon all these. And the holy Lord will come forth with wrath and chastisement, to execute judgment upon the earth." Compare also Psalms of Solomon 17:21,42, Testament of the XII Patriarchs, Judah 24:6, etc. "Woe to the nations that rise up against my race. The Lord Almighty will take vengeance of them in the day of judgment" (Judith 16:17).

"But the righteous shall live for ever and the Lord is their reward, and the care for them with the Most High. Therefore they shall receive a glorious kingdom and a diadem of beauty from the Lord's hand" (Book of Wisdom 3:15 f.). "Then shall the city that is now invisible appear; and the land which is now concealed be seen. And whosoever is delivered from the predicted evil shall see My wonders" (2(4) Esdras 7:27).

That this is one general strain of the literature of this era is beyond dispute. It is the literature of longing. It is the *cri de coeur* of captives who hail the day of release and reinstatement from afar. It is predominantly the creation of long-constricted emotion blazing out in wild and hungry exultation which compensates by its fierceness for the gruelling torment of the present. Never perhaps have the writers of any age revealed the raw heart of their people in such stridently passionate terms.

Yet there is also in this literature the occasional sigh of those who are weary of thoughts of war, vengeance and the delights of victory. Again and again the meek man is heard to ask for nothing more than the peace of God. "But with the righteous He will make peace, and will protect the elect, and mercy shall be upon them. And they shall all belong to God, and they shall be prospered, and they shall all be blessed. And He will help them all, and light shall appear unto them and He will make peace with them" (1 Enoch 1:8).

It is within the compass of such a turgid era and in the context of such a passionate and volcanic literature that the idea of resurrection comes to its most absolute development. It is not found there as the sole expression of the hope beyond death, any more than the Messianic kingdom is the sole expression of the national hope of Israel. But it has become the native expression of man's ultimate expectation, and its effects on life, literature and theology are radical.

These general characteristics of a period which ranges into the New Testament era cannot be swept aside as irrelevant. The letters A.D. are a useful convention. But they do not mark a break in history. It is not possible for any Canute to halt the waves of a people's life and thought at a selected point.

If the background of the Gospel is important to the understanding of the Gospel, it must be recognised that

that background is not only the Old Testament, but what was done and thought by people to whom the Old Testament was already history and the New Testament inconceivable. There is no hiatus in history and in this world even revelation has a history.

CHAPTER FIVE

HISTORY TRANSFIGURED

THE road through Palestine led south and west to Egypt, north and east to Mesopotamia, north and west to Asia Minor and Europe. Every great imperial power discovered the need to command it.

Sooner or later the armies of Egypt, Assyria, Babylonia, Persia, Greece and Rome marched and fought in the arena between the Negeb and Syria. To a unique degree geography dictated history in this small country on the cross-roads between the seats of military and political might, "the high-road of civilisations and the battlefield of empires".

From the days of David its inhabitants were avid for independence and dreamed of a peculiar greatness in the teeth of the adverse forces of geography and history. All that was possible politically was a fitful self-respect in one, brief, fortunate interval when the giants had exhausted themselves. It began about 1000 B.C. and disintegrated in painful stages to its irrevocable term in 586 B.C. Its days were very strictly numbered, like the days of an Indian summer.

But there came a second though even more forlorn chance when Roman power began to lay a restraining hand on the Seleucid successors of Alexander the Great. In 169 B.C. the Maccabean Revolt against Antiochus IV seemed to some a trumpet-blast announcing the age of promise at last. But the Hasmonaean kingdom was a surd, a sport of history. Not even fanatical heroism and the acme of desperate hope could forge a new destiny for such a land at such a time.

Yet the sticks and stones of fate were powerless to splinter the vision which gave the sons of Israel zest for life. Rather the story of 200 B.C. to A.D. 70 is of a dream which was more vivid than reality, an ecstasy more tangible than history itself.

History is continuous, yet even the most encyclopaedic mind cannot view it as a panorama any more than a book can be read without passing from chapter to chapter. It is a drama with its various acts and, within the acts, scenes which are intelligible in themselves as mere incidents cannot be.

The intelligible period before us is from the destruction of Jerusalem by Nebuchadnezzar in 586 B.C. to the Jewish War and the destruction of Jerusalem by the Romans in A.D. 70. It includes the period of Persian ascendancy from 549 to 331 B.C. and of Greek dominion under Alexander's Ptolemaic (Egypt) and Seleucid (Syria) successors to 65 B.C., and the arrival of Pompey's legions heralding imperial Rome. With the exception of 70 paradoxical years it is an era of changing masters but unchanging servitude.

All is as it were a scene within the act of history which is the rise and decline of Mesopotamian prowess in world politics. For even the empires of Greece and Rome are involved in the dissolution of the East as a focus of power, as much as in the creation of a western centre of civilisation.

But viewed from a distance and not neglecting its ruined aspirations, its intrigues, its baleful compromises with mere might, its piteous yearnings for the success it courted and abhorred at the same time, this was for Israel an age of glory and not only when martyrdom was the price of patriotism.

Consider the sheer actual achievement in the terms that speak of renown and success to other peoples. Jerusalem is destroyed; the walls are rubble; the temple is open to the sky; the surrounding country supports an impoverished and politically despondent peasantry; leadership and hope are gone.

Yet, from the inspiration of exiles, the climate of hope returns. The temple is restored; the walls rebuilt; a community of fifty thousand is governed, disciplined and harnessed to a creative purpose. In due course revolt is not only possible but successful and for 70 years this Jerusalem is once more the capital of an Israelitish kingdom.

The period of independence was 134 to 63 b.c. The kingdom reached its widest extent under Alexander Jannaeus, High Priest and King (102–75). For a few years his territories were almost as large as those of Solomon had been.

But this was not the kingdom of Israel's dream—nor the king. Jannaeus had the appetite for greatness and was miraculously successful. But his cruelty (he is reported to have crucified 800 of his opponents), and his cynical disregard for the sanctity of his office, increased party bitterness within the kingdom. He died execrated and unlamented.

Conquest and independence did not bring with them any indication that hope was near fulfilment for the sons of Israel. "Under the blast of Jewish conquests, civilisation in Palestine withered away. Where there had been prosperous cities were heaps of ruins. Fields went back to brushwood, and roaming bands of marauders had free course in the land. Such a state of things marked the zenith of Hasmonaean power."*

Civil strife and the rise of Rome to imperial stature

* Edwyn Bevan, *Jerusalem under the High Priests*, p. 128.

brought a speedy end to national independence. Rome's policy to extend her dominion to the Euphrates did not allow of internecine war in Judea. The temple mount was captured in 63; twelve thousand Jews are said to have died and Pompey entered the Holy of Holies to wonder and despise.

Rome was master. A hundred years of restive servitude brought the climax of four hideous years of the Jewish War. Titus, after a five months' siege, captured Jerusalem in A.D. 70 and found a civil war still in progress in the upper city. Thousands had perished and many thousands were captured and sold as slaves all over the world. This was the end—but already a new beginning had been made.

This record of heroism and hatred, pathos, intrigue, stupidity and all the stuff of history, is not the legacy of these times to the advancing story of the human race. Out of these frantic centuries, incredible as it seems, comes a contribution to the spiritual stature of man whose character is unique. From this volcanic depth erupts a splendour. A torch was lit which is as a pillar of fire in the night of man's groping towards the destiny which he cannot see but which yet lures him on.

It is the literature not the history of this epoch that still speaks to humanity. The ideas and ideals of the time are more potent than the events. History was the anvil but that which was being shaped was not empire—or the power which builds the kingdoms of this world. From the exile to the fall of Jerusalem in A.D. 70 the Jews created out of their agonies a super-history. The flesh became word. The heard melodies were but an accompaniment of those strains unheard but so much sweeter.

Take a people whose God is holy, righteous and absolute and whose history is played out as the pawn of pagan powers, a people who believe themselves a chosen race and who suffer all the extremes of oppression and degradation century after century. What is to be the issue of this contest between faith and fact? Shall not what is called reality finally abolish the insubstantial dream? Must they not bow to the imperious will of ineluctable events at last?

Even the peoples that attained vast empire, whose great ones carved their glories in stone and whose gods were accorded names above every name in view of palpable triumphs which history could record, even these went down before the fact of time. Such were Egypt, Babylon, Persia. How should Israel, a pigmy among the sons of Anak, endure and succeed? Only because history is not acknowledged as final and a divine history is being written by the hand that also writes the perishable record of this world. Israel is the hero in God's history book, the last and the greatest.

It may seem that we have wandered from our precise subject, but the truth is that though we have isolated the idea of resurrection for our investigation, we cannot separate it from its climate in history and in the history of ideas. Our outline of this period and of the ethos of Israel throughout it provides the setting in which the idea of resurrection comes into its own. When you are being killed all the day long and refuse to die, the only explanation is resurrection. It makes endurance possible and at the same time provides a motive for it.

It would take us too far afield to begin to indicate in detail the development that took place in Jewish thought about the Kingdom, the Messiah and eschatology in general. All were modified by the same inexorable pressure of events and by the advance and recession of the tides of hope which lap the shores of a people's soul.

These hopes, which are the real legacy of Israel to the world, fluctuated between history and super-history. They are neither purely material nor purely ethereal. They are a congeries of crass fanaticism and sublime aspiration which flourish, like tares and wheat, in the same field.

The whole of Apocalyptic literature from Daniel and the Apocalypse of Weeks, written about 160 B.C., through to the Similitudes of Enoch and the books assigned to the second half of the first Christian century are punctuated by shouts of defiance at the actual course of history and vehement expressions of hope in divine redintegration.

At times in the literature of the period the kingdom longed for is a kingdom like that of David, only more extensive and illustrious. At other times this is viewed as a discarded and despised delusion, not for Israel for whom more lasting and heavenly glories are laid up. When history seems to smile on the prospect of earthly dominion for Israel, her mentors rush to this door of hope to lead the people through to the destiny promised by pre-exilic and exilic seers. When the next blow is struck and the expectation of worldly prestige is seen to be a chimera, a door of hope is opened in heaven through which the pent-up ardours of the age are released in visions of divine consolation for Israel and condign punishment for the nations.

Consentaneously, the figure of the deliverer is sometimes a hero-king or hero-priest who will lift up Israel's head among the heathen. When all kinglets and priestlings prove broken reeds, hope fastens on the heaven-appointed representative whose supernatural endowments usher in the kingdom which has no end and seals the doom of Israel's oppressors.

It is idle to look for systematic orthodoxy among the varied and sometimes contradictory forms in which the hopes of this era are expressed. Hope weaves its own garments and is not subject to logical conventions. Thus, regarding the inauguration of the new era there is sometimes no mention of a king, as in Daniel and Enoch 1–36. In the Psalms of Solomon a Davidic Messiah is expected. In the Dead Sea Scrolls (Manual of Discipline, 9. 10 f.), the Testament of Levi, Jubilees xxi, two Messiahs— a priestly and a Davidic—are looked for. There is growth but not uniform development.

Again, the doctrine of resurrection though present in Daniel is absent from the Psalms of Solomon and the first part of Enoch while in some books, notably the book of Wisdom, there is a fully developed doctrine of immortality.

We are in an age of religious creativity almost without parallel. Aspiration bodies forth its secrets with all the unchartered liberty which the unwritten future can afford to those who believe the best is yet to be.

A great authority comments on the unsystematic nature of these beliefs and warns that "we must beware of trying to make clear and systematic that which often remains vague and obscure. It is a temptation which has not always been resisted; and yet it is only necessary to glance at the more detailed descriptions of such major events as the fate of the dead while awaiting judgment, the coming of the Messiah, and the final destiny of the wicked, to discover many diverse conceptions and even speculations. No doubt all these variations were equally acceptable so long as they could find a place in the general programme which proved to be extremely comprehensive. Possibly the only thing which all these Messianic writers had in common was the liveliness of their hope and the eagerness with which they awaited its fulfilment."*

In the latter part of our period there is a strange oxymoron in the attitude to historical events. History is both courted and despised, expected to justify Israel at last and disdained as the sphere of pagan arrogance. It is as if history had a body and a soul. Each was alternatively loved and hated but no true dichotomy was possible however longed for. So the kingdom is "here" or "there", or "here" and "there", but never "now". The Messiah is man or superman but always to come. This earth will flourish beyond belief or a new earth will come into being in which righteousness shall dwell. Israel shall be liberated by revolt or by supernatural intervention, by arms or by piety, by the sword of the Maccabees or by the sword of God or both.

Toynbee calls such a transfiguration of the historical context in the thought of a people by the name of etherealisation and describes it as "a transference of energy or shift of emphasis from some lower sphere of being or action to a higher sphere".† Again, he speaks of Futurism and Anarchism as "both alike attempts to break with an irksome present by taking a flying leap out of it into another reach of the stream of time without abandoning the plane of mundane life on earth" (6. 97).

Such a climate of thought could not exist apart from the idea of resurrection, especially where the body–soul anthropology of Hebrew tradition persisted. A future beyond the span of life or a future in a new world was not conceivable to traditional Jewish thought except in terms of resurrection.

That Hellenism with its body-and-soul anthropology

---

* C. Guignebert, *The Jewish World in the time of Jesus*, pp. 134–5.
† *Study of History*, chap. 3, p. 193.

had also made headway among the Jews of the inter-Testamental period is evident and we must turn to this in the next chapter. But resurrection is a prior conception to immortality in the development of Judaism. It remains strongly entrenched into the first century of the new dispensation.

In this realm it is impossible to separate causes and consequences completely. Resurrection in such a setting is both a hope and an incentive, a goal which is ardently desired and an inspiration by which men live. This is not the realm of logic but of faith. Men did not reason in the fashion A, therefore B, therefore C. They asserted A and B and C and were not daunted by rational incongruity. Their faith was in a God to whom all things were possible.

CHAPTER SIX

THE LURE OF IMMORTALITY

No man or nation or race is an island, Israel and Judaism not excepted. Hebrew religion comes up out of the mists of Semitic tribal life, showing the unmistakable marks of its origin. When it takes its place in the light of history, it lives by drawing sustenance from its surroundings according to the needs of its own nature. Neighbours and conquerors alike contribute to its growth. Only gradually does it attain such self-consciousness as enables it to accept and reject according to a known principle of its own uniqueness.

By 331 B.C. Alexander the Great had conquered Asia Minor, Syria, Egypt, Palestine and Persia and initiated his programme for the Hellenization of the world. The Jewish faith had reached years of discrimination and was aware of its own identity. But the process of assimilation which was the principle of life itself did not cease.

Judaism was therefore racked by the question as to what her indebtedness should be to this latest and least uncongenial historical environment. How far the process went in the Dispersion is marked by the fact that the Old Testament was translated into Greek (begun in Alexandria about 250 B.C.) and it was impossible to accept the tongue and wholly reject the culture. When Greek was heard in the synagogues of the Dispersion, Hellenism had already won a notable entry to the sanctum of Judaism.

Hellenism was not a way of thought but a way of life.

If Alexander himself never dreamed of making all his subjects philosophers, it is certain that his successors could form no such conception. What was hoped for, and attained in no small degree, was that the nations of the empire should begin to learn how to live as the Greeks did. As Athens was the education of Greece, so Greece should be the education of the world.

It was sad but natural that the outward signs of such a manner of life, the gymnasia, the libraries, the political institutions, should come to be regarded as the essence of this education. The vision of Alexander faded into the light of common day in the eyes of later generations. As most imperial powers discover, it is easy to export institutions but not to transmit life.

To many in Palestine the Greek way of life was not undesirable. At the same time, those who knew the gift God had bestowed on His chosen people knew also that Israel had no need of Hellenistic amenities. To the young and the politic the new way of life was the way ahead. But the devout remembered the warnings of the prophets and were zealous for the separation of God's people from contamination. They stood in the tradition of Elijah and the great ones who had recalled Israel from her whoredoms to the covenant of God.

On the plane of history this crisis came to its head in the Maccabean Revolt. Israel cast out paganism and was rewarded with independence—for a time. But the spirit of the new age was not so readily exorcised, even from Judea.

Hellenism was a way of life. But every way of life depends upon a way of thought. And nowhere is the contrast between Hellenism and Judaism more clearly visible than in matters of anthropology, or ideas about the nature of man, and eschatology, or ideas of the final destiny of

man. Roughly, for traditional Judaism man is a body–
soul unity: for Hellenism he is a soul in a body. For the
one, hope beyond the grave at this stage of Jewish development must take the form of resurrection; for the other,
immortality. The surest sign that Hellenistic thought
was assimilated by Judaism is the unmistakable presence of
incongruities in the literature of this age which are due to
the fascination of Greek ideas of the soul and immortality.

So notable are these evidences that scholars are accus-
tomed to distinguish between Hellenistic and Palestinian
Judaism when dealing with the literature of the period.
The books which form the Old Testament Apocrypha
were mostly written in the last two centuries B.C. The
majority are deemed to be of Palestinian origin. The remaining literature which ranges in date from the Maccabean period to the end of the 1st century A.D. and is sometimes referred to as Pseudepigrapha, is generally separated
into Palestinian and Hellenistic. Thus the Sibylline
Oracles Books III, IV and V; 3 and 4 Maccabees; 2
Enoch and 3 Baruch, are regarded as Hellenistic in
origin while the rest are Palestinian.

But it would be a vast mistake to regard this division
purely as a geographical one. Most of this literature is
anonymous or pseudonymous and the criteria used to
distinguish the documents are (1) language, some being
originally in Hebrew or Aramaic and some originally in
Greek and (2) whether the documents show greater or
less familiarity and sympathy with Hellenistic ideas.
Those that give evidence of openness to Greek thought
are surmised to belong to the Dispersion rather than to
Palestine. But it would be rash to assume that there were
no Hellenisers in Judea (cf. 1 Macc. 1:11–15 and the
growth of the Sadducean party) and no conservative Jews
in the Dispersion (exiles can be fiercely patriotic).

However, the main point is that Greek and Hebrew notions of man and the life beyond the grave meet and strive and survive in the literature of the age in all those ways that we should expect—conservative Judaism, Hellenism and the various incompatible amalgams of both.

This may be illustrated as follows. Ecclesiasticus or the Wisdom of Ben Sira, composed about 150 B.C., was apparently written to show the superiority of Hebrew wisdom to Greek. As regards the future life it reveals what may be called the traditional Old Testament eschatology. Man's expectation is the grave. This is true also of the Books of Tobit, Judith and Baruch. There is little if any awareness of Hellenism as a real threat to Judaism. Israel possesses her own soul.

"Give and take and beguile thy soul; for there is no seeking of luxury in the grave. All flesh waxeth old as a garment; for the covenant from the beginning is 'Thou shalt die the death'. As of the leaves flourishing on a thick tree, some it sheddeth, and some it maketh to grow; so also of the generations of flesh and blood, one cometh to an end, and another is born. Every work rotteth and falleth away, and the worker thereof shall depart with it" (Ecclus. 14:16–19).

In 2 Maccabees which purports to be a summary of a five-volume history written by Jason of Cyrene (2 Maccabees 2:23) and is dated about 50 B.C. we have an extension of eschatology in the congenial direction, that is in accordance with the demands of the Old Testament type of anthropology. Hades is prepared for the wicked and is only the temporary abode of the good; they will partake in bodily resurrection to newness of life. There is no mention of the resurrection of apostates (contrast Dan. 12:2 in this respect).

In chapter seven of this book in which legend is more conspicuous than history, a mother and her seven sons suffer torture and death rather than eat swine's flesh at the command of the king, Antiochus Epiphanes. The first son was fried to death. The second also "underwent the next torture in succession, as the first had done. And when he was at the last gasp, he said, 'Thou, miscreant, dost release us out of this present life, but the King of the world shall raise up us, who have died for his laws, unto an eternal renewal of life'.

"And after him was the third made a mocking-stock. And when he was required, he quickly put out his tongue, and stretched forth his hands courageously and nobly said, 'From heaven I possess these; and for his laws' sake I contemn these; and from him I hope to receive these back again', insomuch that the king himself and they that were with him were astonished at the young man's soul, for that he nothing regarded his pains.

"And when he too was dead, they shamefully handled and tortured the fourth in like manner. And being come near to death he said then, 'It is good to die at the hands of men and look for the hopes which are given by God, that we shall be raised up again by him; for as for thee, thou shalt have no resurrection unto life' " (2 Maccabees 7:7–14).

2 Baruch which belongs to the end of the 1st century A.D. raises the question, "In what shape will those live who live in thy day?" The answer is given that "the earth will then assuredly restore the dead, which it now receives, in order to preserve them, making no change in their form but as it has received, so it will restore them, and as I delivered them unto it, so also will it raise them" (2 Baruch 49:2–4).

Turning now to evidence of Hellenistic influence, the

Book of Wisdom, assigned to 100–50 B.C., is an excellent example. It shows a belief in the pre-existence of the soul. It teaches a doctrine of immortality attained through acquaintance with wisdom here on earth. It regards the body as evil and subject to corruption; it is the soul that is precious and persists—"The souls of the righteous are in the hand of God," etc. (Wisdom 3:1–9).

Commenting on the salient features of the Book of Wisdom, Pfeiffer states that the author is a precursor of Philo of Alexandria (a contemporary of Paul) in combining the Jewish religion with Greek Philosophy. "The teaching about the retribution of individual Jews after death is more Greek than Hebrew. Logically—but (alas!) not generally—notions about the future life should be based on the ideas of the elements constituting a human being, as in Eccl. 12:7 which refers to Gen. 2:7. In attempting to combine the Hebrew notion of man (body and spirit, Gen. 2:7) with the Greek notion (body, soul and spirit: cf. 1 Thess. 5:23), the author on the one hand asserted that man consists of a physical and a spiritual element (1:4; 2:3, 15:8), but on the other used indiscriminately the Greek terms pneuma, psyche, and nous (mind) which presupposed the Greek anthropology. Moreover, he recognised with Plato that the souls are pre-existent (8:20) and pressed down by the corruptible body (9:15)."[*]

After referring to the Wisdom of Solomon, D. S. Russell in his *Between the Testaments* (pp. 24 f.) continues: "At least two other books express this same belief. In 1 Enoch 91–104 (*c.* 164 B.C.) the writer refutes the Sadducean view that there is no difference between the lot of the righteous and the lot of the wicked beyond death (102:6–8, 11) and affirms on the contrary that 'all goodness and joy and glory are prepared' for the souls of the

[*] *The Interpreter's Bible*, Vol. 1 (1952), p. 407.

righteous (102:3). They shall live and rejoice and their spirits shall not perish (103:4). So also in the Book of Jubilees (*c.* 150 B.C.) the righteous pass at once after death into the blessedness of immortality—'Their bones shall rest in the earth, and their spirits shall have much joy' (23:31)."

From this point of view the most interesting document is 2 (4) Esdras (3–14) which "reflects the tragic aftermath of the destruction of Jerusalem in A.D. 70". Here the visions and talks with an angel about the things to come show a conglomeration of belief about the nature of man and his final destiny.

The body is regarded as corruptible and yet the conception of resurrection is present. Though the author never speaks of the resurrection of the body, he visualises an intermediate state after death in terms requiring a quasi-material body which is nevertheless fit for entry into the new world that is to be created. It is not clear whether the new life begins for the individual after death or after the judgment.

Other parts of this book display the traditional belief in the (general) resurrection of the body. The Messianic Age is preceded by a time of woes. Thereafter Messiah reigns for 400 years at the end of which period all things die (including Messiah) and there is a seven days' silence. Then all are resurrected for the judgment and the righteous enter the New Age.

When we consider the impact of Hellenism on Judaism as represented in the main sects of the inter-Testamental period, we are forced to conclude that the idea of immortality made steady headway till it was possible to associate both without any oppressive sense of incongruity.

According to Josephus, the Pharisees first became prominent in conflict with John Hyrcanus (134–104

B.C.). They were staunch resisters of the growing influence of Hellenism. Their strength came from devotion to the Law, written and oral, which they specialised in applying to everyday life through the agency of the synagogues both in Palestine and in the Dispersion.*

As regards belief in a future life Josephus says (in *B. J.* 2. 8. 14) that the Pharisees thought that "every soul is incorruptible, but that only the souls of the good pass over to other bodies, and those of the wicked are chastened with eternal punishments".

Whether this is simply a manner of expressing belief in a bodily resurrection or indicates a belief that each soul will receive a new body on the other side of death (compare 1 Cor. 15) is difficult to decide, but the influence of Hellenism is patent, at least in the manner of expression, while in the New Testament the Pharisaic belief in the resurrection is fundamental.

The Sadducees were in origin aristocratic and their main concern appears to have been (as appears in the New Testament) to maintain the *status quo* or at least to avoid violent and intemperate reaction to the political and social structure. They believed in the Law but rejected the oral traditions and, whereas the Pharisees dominated the synagogue, the Sadducees supported the centralised worship at the Temple and the High Priest and his family were of this party.

Josephus (*B. J.*, 11. 8. 14) says they denied fate in human affairs, repudiated the doctrine of immortality and of rewards and punishments after death. In the Gospels they argue against the resurrection (Mark 12:18). Paul sets the Pharisees against the Sadducees on this matter in Acts 23:6.

The Essenes had much in common with the Pharisees

* See *Ant.*, 13. 10. 5–7, sects 288–99.

and it has been thought that these two parties originally diverged from one. Pliny the Elder (*Nat. Hist.*, v, 17) speaks of a strictly ascetic brotherhood of about 4000 living near the western shore of the Dead Sea who spent much time in group study of the Scriptures. Josephus (*B. J.*, 2. 8. 10) tells us that they thought bodies corruptible but souls immortal, and "when they are set free from the bonds of the flesh they then rejoice and mount upwards as if released from a long bondage. They also think, like some of the Greeks, that good souls have their habitations beyond the Ocean ... while they allot to bad souls a murky and cold den, full of never-ceasing punishments."

The Zealots according to Pfeiffer are "the heirs of the Maccabees". They are properly regarded as intense Jewish patriots who conceived themselves to be devoutly religious in their aspirations. Their fanatical opposition to the Roman overlord was based on zeal in obedience to the Law.

Josephus tells us they loved liberty, called no man lord, and regarded God as their only king (*Ant.*, 18. 1. 6, sect. 23). He adds that they thought light of pain and had no fear of dying. As regards their beliefs they "agree in all things with the Pharisaic notions".

The discovery of the Dead Sea Scrolls in 1947 has led to much speculation on the nature of the Qumran community. Many think they must be related to, if not identified with, the Essenes. They appear to have practised group study of the Scriptures and to have many points of comparison with the Pharisees in relation to the Law and Sabbath observance. By the end of the 1st century B.C. they have become "a cooled-down apocalyptic sect", believing that the end of the age was near.*

* *The War of the Sons of Light and the Sons of Darkness.*

The Qumran community believed in the survival of the souls of righteous people. They "will stand eternally in the glow of the Perfect Light till the end of the time". There is no definite statement of belief in the resurrection of the body.*

It is worth noting that while a general conclusion on tendencies is possible without precise knowledge of the date and place of inter-Testamental literature, the period presents enormous problems when considered in detail. To trace the development of thought regarding the Messiah, the coming of the Kingdom and its nature, the judgment and the fate of the righteous and the wicked, with any certainty, would require a knowledge of the date and provenance of particular books which is not possible to us at present.

Notice has already been taken of the fact that the division of some of the literature into Palestinian and Hellenistic is precarious, though the best we can do. The same must be said about dating. There are few substantial fixed points of reference and the best that can be said very often is that if A was written about such and such a time, then B is to be dated before (or after) A. The scope for division of opinion on details is therefore wide.

This, of course, applies to the New Testament as well. If, for example, we knew when the first draft of Luke–Acts was written and for what purpose, we should be well on the way to a consistent exposition of the Apostolic Age.

Lacking such precise data, we are often at the mercy of pre-conceived theory and the temptation to fit the pieces into the theory is great. This is particularly obvious in discussions of such subjects as Son of Man, Messiah,

* See e.g. *A Guide to the Scrolls*, by Hanson, Leaney and Posen (1958), chap. 9.

Kingdom, and Judgment, which start from pre-suppositions derived, for instance, from a particular theory of the person and place of Christ in the divine plan.

It is necessary, therefore, to point out that these illustrations are samples taken from the literature of the whole period which covers a range of about 250 years. But this does not invalidate the argument which is simply that Hellenism had a modifying influence upon the development of Judaism as far as the doctrines of man and the life beyond the grave are concerned.

The scope of thought is widened. Sheol, resurrection and immortality are the pivots upon which speculations on things to come revolve. Sheol itself is no longer the Sheol of the Old Testament and the resurrection of the body is an idea in competition with the idea of the immortality of the soul.

Judaism bequeaths to Christianity the contest between the rigorously Hebraic idea of resurrection and the Hellenistic conception of immortality. Christianity in its turn gives new impetus to the idea of resurrection, but is unable to resolve the conflict even in its initial stages (i.e. in the New Testament) and even to the present.

CHAPTER SEVEN

CITY OF MANSOUL

In the inter-Testamental era Judaism was fighting for survival on two main fronts—political and cultural. Because it was shot through with a kind of theocratic idealism which gave it its peculiar identity, its future could only be conceived of, firstly, as a kingdom of which the ultimate king was the God of Israel, and secondly, as a culture which distinguished it from every other culture. "Ye shall be holy for I am holy."

These are the facts which made the Maccabean War inevitable. In the mid-2nd century B.C. the existence of Israel as a nation and Judaism as a culture were both threatened. Dominion by a pagan monarch (Antiochus IV) and infiltration of a pagan ethos (Hellenism) had to be resisted if the ideals of Judaism were to persist.

The frustrations that attended even the most heroic and devout attachment to these ideals produced the climate in which apocalyptic was born and in which eschatology became a primary focus of hope. Resurrection was a natural and necessary scene in the apocalyptic drama of things to come.

But so far we have been dealing only with the public aspect of the subject: we must now attend to the private. In so doing let us first of all make clear to ourselves the impossibility of excogitating the thoughts and motives of any individual adherent of Judaism in this period, except in so far as they can be deduced from a particular document. What we aim at rather is some notion of the kind of questions and answers which men as men were concerned with in this age, and particularly in their bearing on the growth of the primary idea of resurrection.

Belief in resurrection became a psychological and theological necessity of the period. It is present in the literature not only because it was essential to the aspirations of Judaism, but also because it was a possible and congenial expression of the aspirations of individual Jews. It was exalted into prominence by the exigencies of both national and personal idealism. Hope could not live without it in that age, neither the hope of Judaism nor the hope of individual Jews.

The problems of a religious man's future arise out of his present as a man who believes in God. They take the form of a demand for assurance that his union with God cannot be broken, in conflict with awareness that death is at least a form of dissolution. They are shaped by the fact of life's instability and incompleteness, on the one hand, and the faith that God must be both righteous and almighty, on the other.

So long as the fact of life's fragmentariness is accepted unreflectedly and the conception of God is not completely an ethical one, the demand for assurance does not project itself beyond death, except in the form of an existence in Sheol or Hades or in the continuing life of man's offspring.

Death is not a penalty for sin in this era but a necessity of nature. It cannot be interpreted as a means of discrimination between the righteous and the wicked, nor can it lead to a hope which provides a recompense to the good for their misfortunes in life or a foreboding of punishment for the deeds of evil men. To all indiscriminately it is a fact to be accepted as the universe is accepted. The wise woman of Tekoa states it in its stark and pragmatic simplicity. "We must die, and are as water spilt on the ground, which cannot be gathered up again" (2 Sam. 14:14).

This is true of practically the whole of the Old Testament era, except that towards the end of it new questions are being asked which as yet cannot be answered. The era of fatalistic acceptance of life's obvious limits is passing; the righteousness and therefore the omnipotence of God are being progressively moralised.

We therefore find a period in which the tension between faith and fact is at its maximum. More is being demanded of life, in the sense that man is no longer content with the natural pessimistic conclusion to the drama of his own existence. More is being demanded of God, in the sense that deep and searching questions of an existential nature are not silenced by the answer of omnipotence. And still the fact of immortality or some form of illumination which brightens for man the other side of death has not yet arrived.

This is the period of poignancy so well represented in Job and the Psalms, both of which reflect the despair and the aspiration inseparable from the dark night of tension. Why is it better never to have been born? Why is man doomed to Sheol? Even within his short life on earth, why is man born to trouble? Why is there no guarantee that goodness fares better than wickedness in the long run? Why should a man not question his God? And if he does, why does God not answer him? Why is Sheol the "land of forgetfulness" where "thoughts perish" and God is not present? Should not God think of His servants even when they have gone to Sheol?

Job is urgently conscious of the need for some assurance from the other side of the grave to sustain him in the ordeal of this present life. But no such assurance is known.

"If I look for Sheol as my house,
   if I spread my couch in darkness,
If I say to the pit, 'You are my father',
   and to the worm, 'My mother', or 'My sister',
   Where then is my hope?"

(Job 17:13–15 (R.S.V.))

Such an interim of agony makes it imperative that faith in the end should modify fact, for Sheol is becoming no longer psychologically believable. It must give way to a conception which will justify the faithful servant of God in his faithfulness in the last resort, and also vindicate the righteousness and omnipotence of God as an object of worship.

This can happen in two ways—by an extension of union with God into or beyond Sheol, or by a reinstatement of man in a revised and righteous order of the world. In other words, personal religion at this stage demanded resurrection or immortality or some effective modification of the thought of life beyond death which allowed man to continue to believe in the righteousness and power of God and the worthwhileness of personal piety.

Two forces native to the Hebrew tradition pressed in the direction of resurrection as the obvious enlargement for the aspirations of the devout. Firstly, the fact that Hebrew anthropology remained undeveloped and thus incapable of the conception of disembodied spirit necessary to the idea of immortality. A shade was not a disembodied spirit but the shadow of a man. Enriched life beyond the grave meant the survival of man and not only his shadow and for this the grave must give up the body, without which there is no man.

In the second place the corporate hopes of Israel embodied in the conception of a kingdom on earth for the righteous, found natural representation in the idea of the raising of the saints to enjoy the time of bliss. In Isaiah 26:19 (dated 200 B.C. on) this makes its appearance as a hope or prayer confined to individual Israelites who deserved it. It would fittingly be desired for the martyrs of the faith (cf. 2 Macc. 7:11; 14:46 where martyrs are expected to receive again those parts of their bodies which have been mutilated).

From this it is an easy transition to the idea that if the good are raised to enjoy the reward of their faithfulness, the evil may also be raised to meet their deserts in punishment. Daniel 12:2 (mid-2nd century B.C.) shows this at its inception. The notion is still confined to some Israelites, the very good to be raised to blessedness, the very wicked to punishment. It does not depend on any essential constituent of man as man, but solely upon the action which may be postulated of a God of righteousness such as Judaism revered.

The next stage is the further extension of the idea to embrace the whole of humanity in view of a general judgment. This extension marks the new scope of post-exilic prophecy and apocalyptic.

We have seen, however, that a new path of psychological development was opened up in the persistent environment of Hellenism. If it were possible to get beyond the primitive anthropology of Hebrew thought, this also would be recognised as a means of relieving the spiritual tension of the age. It is recognised by the more reflective writers of the period and the conception of immortality as the destiny of the soul is taken up into the stream of Jewish eschatology.

Such a conception would have satisfied the writer of Job (final form about 350 B.C.?) whose problems are intensely personal and not national. What he cries out for is the assurance that in no circumstance will he be deserted by God. Death is dreadful because it denies this possibility, yet it is better to die if this is so. The writer is aware that he cannot either live or die without being tormented with the fact that his very existence is a relationship to God. He is on the verge of being convinced by a *tour de force* of his own mind that even death would not matter if what he cannot put into words were true.

The literary successors of the author of Job are the writer of the Wisdom of Solomon, and Philo. But here we have quite plainly travelled far along the Hellenistic path. The doctrine of the soul is fully accepted and immortality depends upon its nature. We even find the notion of pre-existence, and this is well beyond the limits of Old Testament teaching.

The Book of Psalms provides a fine range of Hebrew thought from the point of view of personal religion, extending as it does from about 1000 B.C. into the Hellenistic period.

Scholars have distinguished three stages of development. There is the era when Sheol is the accepted destiny of man and when the imagined and undefined power of the dead was dreaded. This is followed by a period when it was believed that Sheol was utterly cut off from the life of man and God. Some think this was due to the prophetic movement after 800 B.C. and the official desire to discourage superstitious rites associated with the dead. Sheol is the land of forgetfulness and impotence: its inhabitants are excluded from God's thoughts. The final stage (300 B.C. on) gives the kind of questing after divine consideration beyond the grave which we note in Job (see especially Psalm 139 and 73). But no firm doctrine of immortality or resurrection is yet achieved.

The use of the Psalms has been a principal means down

to the present day of expressing man's personal and intuitive need for the kind of assurance given in the doctrines of resurrection and immortality. How has this been possible in view of the fact that they are written against a background of an undeveloped anthropology and are bounded by the lack of a full doctrine of life beyond the grave?

H. Wheeler Robinson has pointed out that this is in some measure due to our ability to import into the Psalms the anthropology of our own day. And we can do this readily because we ignore the fact that "soul" in most of the Psalms simply means "life". We invest the term with our own psychological presuppositions and thus extend the scope of the Psalmist's thought to match our own.

This is no doubt true and yet it is also true that the essential needs and aspirations of men are not at the mercy of their anthropological ideas. A man in despair or a man in communion with God can speak from the heart in any age in such a way as to reach the heart in any other. And the Psalms are that kind of literature.

The Psalms do not offer proof: they communicate faith and they do so without imposing restrictions on what that faith may achieve in addition to what it achieved in their own case. Calvin called them "an anatomy of all parts of the soul" and the soul aspires to the limit of assurance.

What this means is that the individual discovers within himself a creative conviction as to his own worth in the eyes of God which compels him to invade the realm of the unseen and eternal for the means of his own sustenance as a living soul here and now. What he has is in the nature of *fiducia* (trust) and not *assentio* (intellectual conviction), not a knowledge of what is to be but an assurance of a present relationship with God which time and death are unable to defy. Whether this will be expressed as resurrection or immortality is a contingent matter. The essence is the assurance.

PART II

THE RESURRECTION FAITH

CHAPTER EIGHT

THE CHRISTIAN CREDO

THE New Testament is initially the literature of a sect which has branched off from Judaism. Very naturally it cannot, at least at first, disown its inheritance. It cannot divest itself of the essential context which is the setting for its distinctive characteristics. The new wine is received into old wine skins because there are no others. The background of Jesus and His disciples is 1st-century Judaism; and 1st-century Judaism is directly descended from the Old Testament and the inter-Testamental religious tradition.

That the New Testament became the basis of a new culture and a new civilisation is true. But this could not be known or expected at the time and it is tendentious to allow the fact to affect our historical investigation.

Conceptions of the Kingdom of God, for example, in the minds of those who heard Jesus, were strictly prescribed. They were such as were possible to people living in that particular tradition and at that particular time. That they were modified in the course of time, by Jesus' teaching and subsequent events or non-events, goes without saying; but they arise from the soil of native Judaism.

It is evident that for some time Christians are regarded as simply a sect of the Jews and so regarded themselves.

If we ask why there is a New Testament the answer is because it was believed that the aspirations of Israel and Israelites were in part realised and in whole guaranteed in Jesus. The Church conceived of itself as the New Israel now living under the terms of the New Covenant. The Old was not rejected; it was fulfilled in the New.

Any attempts that were made later to repudiate the revelation in the Old Testament came to nothing. This was a take-over bid. The Old Testament and the New Testament were bound together into one sacred literature. Yet the superiority of the New to the Old is never in doubt within the new community. Initial reluctance to break with Judaism is not due to any idea that the Law and the Gospel are of equal significance; rather it is because the sphere of the New is regarded initially as the same as that of the Old, but in the New the Old is fulfilled.

The promise of God is to Israel and to Israel alone as far as Judaism is concerned, though Gentiles may consequently benefit. The inclusion of Gentiles by Christianity, the enlarging of the Gospel sphere, is forced upon the Church by the pragmatic fact that some Gentiles do believe and do demonstrate that their belief is effective.

Christianity in spite of itself is not capable of being merely a Jewish sect or of fulfilling only Jewish hopes. There is plenty of evidence in Gospels, Acts and Epistles that this was regarded as an unexpected and even an unwarranted development in its initial stages. The reason for this development lies in what is distinctive in the Christian credo.

When we ask what is the salient and distinguishing feature of the New Testament, remembering that it rises out of the context of Judaism in the 1st century, the answer is not so much in terms of the doctrine of God, or man, or in a superior ethic, although in due course these come to be differentiated and to bear their own distinctive character.

On this matter Klausner's statement, for instance,

could hardly be more categorical: "Throughout the Gospels there is not one item of ethical teaching that cannot be paralleled either in the Old Testament and Apocrypha or in the Talmudic and Midrashic literature near to the time of Jesus."*

But the initial impulse which gives direction to the new movement as one destined to break the bounds of Judaism is faith in a divine event which is embodied in the resurrection of Christ. While other literature of the period is based on the anticipation of future divine events, the New Testament is based on the belief in a past event which theoretically makes future events more definite and inevitable because they are now believed to be in process.

The Church and the Church's literature were created by the belief that Jesus is Messiah risen from the dead and that He will come again in power and glory to continue and conclude His appointed work. The point of view that prompts a dogmatic comment on 2 Thess. 1 : 7–10 to the effect that "There is nothing distinctively Christian in its contents or in its general tone, apart from the fact that the figure of the Messiah is identified with Jesus,"† seems to presuppose that Christianity was distinguished at first by ethical or theological doctrines and not by belief in Jesus as the risen Christ.

But the belief that Jesus has risen from the dead is common to the various New Testament documents and at the same time separates them from other related literature of the period. Christians believed that something which was expected by Jews has now come to pass and its consequences must follow.

Commenting on the thought of the 1st century,

* *Jesus of Nazareth*, p. 384.
† C. H. Dodd, *Apostolic Preaching*, p. 81.

Edwyn Bevan* writes: "The few books of Pharisaic piety that have come down to us—Enoch, The Psalms of Solomon, The Assumption of Moses and others—show us indeed what ideas occupied the minds of writers, but they could not have shown us what we learn from our Gospels: how ideas of this order have permeated the people through and through; how the figure of the Coming King, 'the Anointed One', 'the Son of David', how definite conceptions of the Resurrection, of the Other World, were part of the ordinary mental furniture of that common people which hung upon the words of the Lord."

Making essentially the same point Guignebert† says: "It is no exaggeration to say that just before the birth of Jesus, speculations as to the date and duration of the Messianic reign, the Day of Yahweh, the Resurrection and the Last Judgment, were central in Jewish thought, and occupied the chief place among the politico-religious questions which engrossed the inhabitants of Palestine."

It is important to realise that before the New Testament begins to be created the idea of resurrection as the signal instance of divine intervention is already in mass circulation and the possible permutations of mode, time and place related thereto have already been expressed.

On these matters the New Testament writers have nothing new to contribute unless we regard the expectation of a limited resurrection at the Parousia (1 Cor. 15) as a new variation on the original theme. The variety of expectation is evident in the various documents and the New Testament does not even distinguish itself by erecting an orthodoxy of belief in this matter. Its significance is in another direction, that this divine event has already happened in one, and therefore a unique instance.

* *Jerusalem Under the High Priests*, p. 158.
† *The Jewish World in the Time of Jesus*, p. 151.

If this is so, and this is undoubtedly what the Church believed, it is like a match to tinder. The consequences were bound to be and were in fact explosive.

The fact that the New Testament is punctuated by references to prophecies, now conceived to have been fulfilled or to be due for fulfilment, is incidental evidence of the relation between the Christian *kerygma* and the time-schedule of the New Age. C. H. Dodd speaks of those references as "a piece-meal assertion of the one great fact that the meaning of history is now summed up".*

Now it is true that the Gospel is conceived of as a crisis of history and a crisis of fulfilment. But that it was in terms of "summing-up" is not so evident. It is not easily proved that the conception of things of the end generally involves the idea of timelessness or the end of time as distinct from the end of an age. Nor is it evident that the New Age was not also a new beginning. There are events of the End and these are successive. It is certainly expected that once they are inaugurated they will proceed inexorably but they do proceed—the Day of the Lord, the ingathering of the elect, the general resurrection, the last judgment are all expected before the consummation. "In the Old Testament and Apocalyptic writings the 'last times' by no means always or necessarily imply the end of all things. Although when the last times are to come about is never stated definitely, they are always presented as a process upon which shall follow the inauguration of a new age."†

The literature dealing with the New Age sets forth a programme to be enjoyed by those who enter it, or rather, many attempts are made to sketch the programme, for speculation revelled in the number and order of these

---

* *Apostolic Preaching*, p. 211.
† W. O. E. Oesterley, *The Doctrine of Last Things*, p. 195.

anticipated events. It is not easy to believe that the eschatological expectations of the early disciples (depicted in the
Gospels as participating in the common earthy interpretation of coming events) were expeditiously refined by
faith in the resurrection of Jesus or teaching of a non-
eschatological nature.

In time, of course, this came to pass—when the next
expected eschatological event failed to occur. But initially
the resurrection was conceived as inaugurating the New
Age and so setting in motion the sequence of events belonging thereto. Hope and expectation were not swal-
lowed up in realisation nor, later, was the sense of baffle-
ment at the delay of the Parousia forestalled.

What this amounts to is that the genius of the New
Testament literature lies in the belief that in Jesus who
rose from the dead the New Age has been inaugurated
and the future is now estimated in reference to Him.
"That" which the prophets foretold is now "This" which
is happening and will happen.

The urgency and passion of the New Testament are
due in the first instance not to a profound exposition of
God's love, although that is there. They are due to the
ringing of a strident alarum which marks a crucial initiating hour in world history. Its effect is exhilaration or
terror, according to a man's relationship to the Gospel.
The atmosphere of crisis, destiny and irrevocability is inescapable. It is there on every page. It is there, not as a
future possibility but as a fact, not as a speculation but as
the instant situation since "now" decides (though it does
not obliterate) "for ever".

The belief that Jesus rose from the dead brought to the
fore some germane questions to which there was a prescribed answer. It was the switch which inaugurated an
automatic series of events in terms of the expectations of

the day. For generations Judaism in its apocalyptic aspects had been working out the answers to questions beginning, "What will happen when . . .?" The answers were ready and the belief in the resurrection of Jesus was the psychological "When".

It is true that this belief was not effective for the majority to whom it ought to apply. As a people the Jews would have none of it. This doesn't alter the fact that had they believed, they would have reacted precisely as the primitive Church did. The primitive Church sees itself taking the action that all Israel ought to take. The fact that all Israel does not take it, is a source of bewilderment, especially to Paul.

Let us consider some of these questions which under-lie the literature of the New Testament. If Jesus has risen from the dead, what time is it? By time is meant time on God's calendar, the plan of the ages into which He has divided the history of the world, the plan which Daniel and Enoch, for instance, have laboured to unfold. And the answer (which is oversimplified but is none the less the only possible answer in the circumstances) is that it is the beginning of the times of the end.

If this should be thought an extreme or partisan way of putting it, let it be remembered that it is a live conclusion only for those who believe in the resurrection of Jesus. But it would also have been the conclusion of all who might have believed. Nothing is more certain than that resurrection˙ is the sign that past history is being folded up and the inevitabilities of eschatology are already in progress. "In all contemporary Jewish literature the Resurrection (whether partial or general) is a sign of the inauguration of the new era."*

This, then, is the extent of the crisis and the reason for

* Sanday & Headlam, *Romans,* p. 325 ff.

the passionate urgency which burns throughout the pages of the New Testament. Here it rises in a consuming blaze; there it is somewhat tempered; but always it is insistent and always central. This is a literature of men caught in a paradoxical era of ineffable glory and unutterable darkness. They are immersed in last-minute operations while flames kindle the whole heaven and make night visible. They are in the "now" of salvation. At any instant the "now" will fan out till everything will exemplify the power and glory of God.

But is this not an extreme and partisan conclusion about the state of mind of the primitive Church? What about the Sermon on the Mount, the parable of the Prodigal Son, 1 Corinthians 13? If we admit that Harnack and Glover and others of the Jesus of History school exaggerated the importance of the person and teaching of Jesus in ethical terms, isn't that element none the less present?

Two things are to be said about this. The first is that although the Gospels come first in the New Testament, in their present form at least they are second generation documents. It is the second generation that takes the trouble to write of the earthly life of Jesus. Even so, only Luke is attempting to write biography. In the whole of the rest of the literature there is nothing that would lead us to believe that the interest of the primitive Church in Jesus is concentrated anywhere else than upon His significance as the One who is believed to have died and risen and is due to come again. This is an eschatological interest.

As to the chapter on love in 1 Corinthians , if by Paul, it was written by one who never met Jesus and according to his own confession had little interest in knowing about His earthly life and teaching. It does not extol Jesus as an example. It cannot be gainsaid that Paul's interest in Jesus is primarily fixed on the eschatological significance of His death and resurrection. He has no salient conclusions to draw from the facts of His life, only from the fact that He lived. His thought, more than any other in the New Testament, is schematic, and the scheme is unquestionably eschatological.

That meantime Christians ought to behave well to one another is a truism. But even here ethics derive from eschatology, never vice versa. For him as for all the New Testament writers it is an automatic premise that if the resurrection has taken place, the New Age is come upon the world; new life is the result of that divine event, not of the *imitatio Christi*. It is identification with Christ, not imitation of Christ, that Paul teaches.

The second question to which the answer was prescribed by apocalyptic tradition is: If Jesus has risen from the dead, who is He? To this there could be only one answer. He is Messiah.

We must beware here of the kind of strict logical thinking which is foreign to the era of the New Testament. Two propositions are involved: "Jesus is Messiah because He rose from the dead" and "Jesus rose from the dead because He is Messiah". They are not identical but it is plain that to the writers of the New Testament they are equally tenable and the one may be used to support the other in either order.

To New Testament writers, and to many writers today, it seems a matter of indifference whether we begin with one and go on to the other or vice versa. In the context of faith this would appear to be so. But it is very different if we are making a historical investigation into the question as to how the resurrection faith began. The difference may be seen if we ask, What comes first, faith or fact? It is sometimes forgotten that faith can create its own fact just as surely as fact creates its own faith.

However that may be, the New Testament makes it plain that the automatic answer for the first generation to the question, Who is Jesus? is quite simply and in the first instance, He is Messiah. No one will say that the later books of the New Testament are content with the prescribed answer, still less that this answer is that which has been embodied in the great creeds. But the Church began with this answer. Whether it is possible for the Church to end where it did is another matter.

Finally, there is the question: If Jesus has risen from the dead, what happens next? Again, the answer is automatic, but necessarily in general terms only. He will come as vicegerent of God—soon—and there will follow a Kingdom, a general resurrection, a judgment, in short, events of the New Age. This is the general expectation of New Testament writers. Whether it is primitive and how it arose are intricate matters and the onus of proof is on those who would deny that it is primitive.

In any case, the gap between the resurrection of Christ and the next expected stage of the eschatological programme has created havoc. As it yawned open, bewilderment became more pronounced. There was no provision for such a gap in the predetermined plan of things that belonged to the end, and at first no psychological cushion against the shock.

Once again, the doubts and queries that perplexed the earnest from this cause are scattered throughout the New Testament. The plan has to be re-thought and there is evidence of *ad hoc* teaching designed to allay the anxieties caused by the non-fulfilment of eschatological expectations. The Fourth Gospel in some passages has almost succeeded in transmuting the whole subject into timeless terms, but in others it shows the same bemused pre-occupation with the divine plan of the future as the rest of the literature.

Thus the early eschatological attitude is seen in the expectation of a day in which those who are in the grave will hear the voice of the Son of Man and come forth to the resurrection of life or to judgment (5:28, 29), and the farewell discourse represents Jesus as speaking of His coming again (14:3). On the other hand this Gospel frequently speaks of eternal life as a present possession which is independent of historical contingencies: "He that liveth and believeth on me shall never die" (11:26). "He that believeth on the Son hath everlasting life" (3:36).

There is recognition in the New Testament that "now" is crucially important but not all-important: there is "not yet" (1 John 3:2). And the "not yet" is so long in coming that it may have to be assimilated to a large extent to the "now". That such assimilation was possible and present from the start is not arguable unless we are prepared to justify a transposition of the Fourth Gospel as it now exists from the end of the New Testament era to its beginning and deny that the non-futurist elements in Johannine eschatology are later than those common to the Four Gospels.

It can no longer be doubted that the Fourth Gospel contains authentic historical material or that a strand of this Gospel goes back to native Palestinian sources of an Essene character.* But the present form and ethos of the Gospel cannot be used as it stands to serve the purposes of historical reconstruction of the life and ministry of Jesus

---

* See, for instance, W. F. Albright, "Recent Discoveries in Palestine and the Gospel of St. John" in *The Background of the New Testament and its Eschatology*, W. D. Davies and D. Daube, eds. (C.U.P. 1956).

and analysis of this complicated document is far from being agreed.

J. A. T. Robinson seems prepared to argue that the Parousia idea, which is not present in Jewish eschatology nor based on the word of Jesus when it appears in the Epistles, cannot be traced to Jesus and must therefore have been introduced later through misinterpretation or misdirection of things said by Jesus. It would seem that the only satisfactory hypothesis that would relieve all the dilemmas he faces in his brilliantly-argued book, *Jesus and His Coming*, is that Jesus spoke of the coming Son of Man but did not mean Himself. Because He was accepted as Messiah after His death and had, during His life, spoken of a future event, the disciples, standing now in the post-crucifixion period, were bound to expect that He should come again. This is, in fact, the position of Bultmann. "In the last analysis therefore Jesus himself in his person is the 'sign of the time'. This, however, does not mean that he invites men to believe in himself. He does not, for instance, proclaim himself as Messiah. In fact, he points to the Messiah, the 'Man', as the Coming One distinct from himself."*

In any case, this hitch in the programme of eschatological expectations leaves open two possibilities which were both taken up into the corpus of New Testament faith. The first is a rabid reinforcement of apocalyptism (since the time must always be coming nearer for the delayed event to happen) and the second is the general merging of the doctrine of resurrection (event) with the doctrine of immortality (existence), briefly, Chiliasm and Hellenisation.

On the one hand, time is emphasised and the urgency and crisis atmosphere thus maintained. On the other,

* *Primitive Christianity*, p. 90.

time is discounted and merged with the eternity of immortality. It is the "now" before the next and imminent stage of apocalyptic development, or the "now" of eternal life which is qualitative and not dependent on an eschatological programme. But this takes us beyond our immediate subject.

The New Testament, then, is not a literature which can be dissociated from its immediate environs, any more than New Testament Greek can be differentiated from the living language of the time directed to a particular use. Its distinctiveness is due to the resurrection faith of Judaism brought into focus in the particular belief that Jesus is risen. The New Testament is the written evidence of the specific belief that history has entered its ultimate stage with consequences which are decisive.

As the flesh became word in the inter-Testamental period, so now the word has become flesh. As history initiated a supra-historical faith then, so faith prescribes the conformation of history now. But history does not conform.

CHAPTER NINE

THE UNFORESEEN HIATUS

We have seen that the New Testament exists because of the belief that God has initiated a new stage in His dealings with mankind through Jesus, who is Christ risen from the dead. How is this new conception to be expressed and how will it affect the life and thought of those who accept it? All the material we have on these questions as far as the first fifty years are concerned is in the New Testament.

Every new dynamic conviction is heralded by what has preceded it; otherwise it could never be accepted. But equally a new conviction distrupts the setting into which it is received and comes into conflict with tenets hitherto securely held. It is at once the offspring and enemy of its environment.

Early Christian apologists are thus forced to show that their faith is a culmination of the purpose of God as revealed in the literature and history of Judaism. At the same time they must maintain its distinctiveness and superiority, even if this should ultimately mean disruption of the formal ties between the two faiths.

In addition, the central tenet itself and the expectations it arouses create problems within the new community of believers. They themselves are part of the tradition out of which the new faith has arisen and with which it is in conflict.

The Pauline letters are the earliest literature we have from the pen of a Christian. It used to be assumed that

Paul's life and letters, that is, his activity as a Christian, could be explained as the outcome of a moment of conversion and revelation on the Damascus road. His teaching in his Epistles was regarded as the application of relevant portions of a corpus of divine insight, given to him once for all and disbursed as need arose in the course of his missionary efforts. He himself believed that he received direct divine revelation and expected some of his teaching to be accepted for that reason.

While there is no cause to question the fact that a crisis occurred in his life and thereafter he was Paul the believer in Jesus as the Christ, this was more likely to be the revelation that lights up and gives meaning to what is already there, than the revelation which conveys an absolutely new corpus of doctrine.

The evidence is that his thought prior to the Damascus experience was running in the mould of Jewish expectation of divine intervention and redemption. His belief that Jesus is the Christ galvanised the whole of his thinking. What he had hitherto regarded as certain to happen but not immediate, had suddenly become present reality. He found himself plunged into the eschatological era which he had up to now only anticipated. From now on he behaves with the fervour of one who knows he is living in the last days and the whole force of his previous anticipation of this time is behind his activities.

The fore-known plan of God is now being put into operation. This is the revelation which Paul calls the Gospel and which he is specially appointed to serve, in particular by preaching to the Gentiles, who are now brought within the scope of God's redemption (Rom. 1:16; 2:9–11; 11:24–26; Gal. 3:7–9; etc.). It is the belief in the resurrection of Christ which precipitates this situation and from this point the whole purpose of God is moving to its consummation (Rom. 3:21–24; 5:1–2; 6:3–6; 8:11–12; 1 Cor. 15:12–20; Gal. 3:22–27).

The ramifications of such a comprehensive schema are complex, but there is nothing in Paul's letters (see note at end of chapter) which is not penned with this general prospective of God's intention in view. The urgency of his present situation is created by the belief that Christ is risen and therefore the things of the end have been initiated.

It is to serve this central conviction that he devotes his use of Scriptures. That he started off from a preconceived belief in a plan in which the resurrection as the overt manifestation of divine intervention was crucial is notable in his use of allegory and in the object for which he feels it necessary to quote the Old Testament.

Paul reinterpreted the Old Testament in accordance with the thesis that the eschatological purpose of God is now being actively fulfilled and this itself in turn is the result of his belief that Messiah has appeared. "It was Paul who provided most of the detached exegetical insights which later interpreters tried to systematise. And in his thought we see combined the various lines of exegesis which existed before him. He was thoroughly at home in the world of Jewish rabbinic exegesis and apparently knew something of allegorisation as well. Along with these methods, both of which he probably knew before his conversion, he came to regard the Old Testament as a Christian book when he became a Christian and then 'baptised' into Christianity the exegesis he had known."*

When the apostle uses the Old Testament it is not merely as illustration or argument. It is to give his own eschatological interpretation of the passage and to harness its authority to his own understanding of the eschatologi-

* R. M. Grant, *The Letter and the Spirit*, S.P.C.K., 1957, p. 47.

cal programme. That is to say, he comes to Scripture to confirm conclusions already held. He uses it to approve an argument in support of eschatological convictions. The main thesis on which his life and ministry are based is eschatological and it is normative for his thought.

For instance, both Philo and Paul used the story of Hagar but to different ends. Philo proves that Sarah's children, representing true wisdom, are superior to Hagar's, representing worldly wisdom. He draws the conclusion that sophistry is to be cast out to make room for virtue. The Law is superior to philosophy.

Paul on the other hand sees in Hagar the type of bondage to the Law. Christians are called to be free of the Law, for the period of its dominion is now past. They are the true children of Abraham through belief in Christ (Gal. 4:22–31).

The allegorical method is common to both, but Paul uses it to enhance a conclusion which is directly related to an eschatological conception of Christ's significance. Thus the Scripture can support a conclusion which takes priority in his own mind. Scripture is not itself revelation but its handmaid, though doubtless Paul believed that Scripture enshrined the purpose of God still to be enacted. Priority in importance belongs to the eschatological prospectus which has been inaugurated by the fact that the Messiah has been revealed.

In Romans 4 the main argument is that believing God as Abraham did is the way to "justification". But Paul finds it necessary to extend this in such a way that this belief includes belief in resurrection on the part of both Abraham and the faithful of Paul's day. He does this by maintaining that Abraham's belief in the birth of Isaac and the Christians belief in the resurrection of Jesus are equally belief in a God who brings life from the dead.

Apart from any question this raises about the nature of the resurrection, the latter part of the argument is obviously dictated by the priority which belief in the resurrection of Christ holds in Paul's mind. It is because this is so that he feels the need to say that Abraham did the same kind of thing when he believed in the birth of Isaac.

As far as Paul is concerned, all the mighty acts of God in history, the creation, the deliverance from Egypt, the giving of the Law, the return from the Exile, are equally with the resurrection of Christ demonstrations of the purpose of God. What makes the resurrection unique is a difference in time and significance. It is the preordained last and historically conclusive mighty act of God up to this hour.

It has this significance because the plan of salvation and its fulfilment is fundamental, the prior datum of Paul's thinking, and because he is persuaded that it has in fact taken place. To this extent the faith of a Christian is different from the faith of Abraham. The former is belief that Christ has been raised, the latter that God will fulfil His promise. What they have in common is that both alike are related to the same God who is able to raise the dead. But this description of God is discovered by Paul in the narrative because it is already paramount in his own mind. It is read in before it is read out.

The eschatological programme discernible in the Pauline writings is no different in general outline from that to be found in the inter-Testamental literature. We have no reason to doubt that Paul's general conception of the future was one that was commonly to be found in the Judaism of his day. But his distinction lies in the fact that for him the final stage of this programme is now in operation and that Messiah's role is now more clearly defined. Both these circumstances are due to his belief that Christ has been raised. That which was still to come as far as his fellow Jew is concerned, is in some measure already here and in process for him.

But practical and insistent problems are immediately raised if it is the case that the expected programme is now in operation. Questions that up to this time were hypothetical are now factual. Details that were formerly of subordinate interest in a broad general forecast, now assume formidable proportions and create unforeseen bewilderment. War plans look different once war has been declared; history modifies prophecy.

The most important difficulties arose from the fact that the programme did not proceed according to expectation: it began but it did not proceed. That which "began as an act of God and an accomplished fact only to resolve itself into a process . . . awaits its final consummation in a new act of God, the revelation of His Son in glory".* But the new act is overdue.

Throughout the New Testament one thing above all creates anxiety and uncertainty. It is the delay after the initial act which brought to an end the former age and ushered in the new age. The question is raised in many different forms but it always concerns the hiatus between the resurrection of Christ and the completion of the eschatological programme. Every document in the New Testament is constricted through still unfulfilled hope; some are unable to mute faithless murmurs of impatience. In crude terms, the resurrection of Christ has not yet been followed by the resurrection of the just to enter and enjoy the new age, as it ought to have been (cf. particularly 1 and 2 Thess.; 1 Cor. and 2 Peter).

We are concerned with the problems this created for Paul. These have to do with (1) the meaning of this

* Anderson Scott, *Christianity According to St. Paul*, p. 236

hiatus in the purpose of God and (2) the present status and prospects of those who are Christ's. We shall deal with the former now and the latter in the next chapter.

What was brought to light by the delay in the completion of the eschatological programme was the unpalatable truth that the majority of the chosen people (Israelites) did not see Jesus as their Messiah and that some of the Gentiles did in fact accept Him. This had not been foreseen and is obviously perplexing.

Paul in Romans 9–11 gives an elaborate exegesis of the rejection of Jesus by the Jews which is to his mind at the same time a temporary rejection of the Jews by God. Indeed, if it is to be explained within the eschatological plan, it has to be the latter and it must serve some divine purpose. This purpose Paul sees in terms of his own particular mission—the ingathering of the Gentiles.

This is the unforeseen thing which Paul claims as having been kept by God in His own counsel. It has now been revealed to Paul as a mystery of God's grace. This is a new departure which was kept secret until the very moment it became operative. It is the reason for the hiatus; it explains for Paul the unexpected delay in the consummation of the divine plan. It reveals God as gracious beyond all comprehension, as a God of infinite and unbounded grace. This hiatus, though it involves the temporary casting off of Israel, is properly understood as the occasion for the marvellous extension of God's mercy to all men, thus enhancing the glory of God.

The hope of resurrection and enjoyment of the age to come is therefore no longer confined to Israel and her proselytes. Indeed, the definition of Israel is now to be modified to include those who up to now had no part in the hopes and promises that belonged to the chosen people.

Paul's new definition of Israel is characteristically one which is dictated by this new feature of the eschatological programme. Israel is now those who believe and therefore have been ordained by the secret will of God to inherit the promises. Paul expounds this new proposition in Galatians in an argument which exhibits his rabbinic skill.

The resurrection to life thus becomes a prerogative not of Judaism but of Christianity, not of Jews who obey the Law but of all who believe that Jesus is the Christ. The problem is solved by an extension of the mercy of God but at the expense of those who conceived the whole eschatological scheme in the first place, the natural children of Abraham. The Church is now the Israel of God.

The point has been made recently by the Jewish scholar Prof. Hans Joachim Schoeps, who says that by the use of typological argument "Paul opens the long line of ecclesiastical authors who have denied to the Jewish people their election privileges and promises, transferring them to Christianity as the new Israel of God by the simple device of typological-allegorical exegesis".*

This solution of the problem created by the delay in the Parousia was not initially acceptable, but two facts were on its side, the protraction of the delay itself and the growth of the Gentile church. It left unsolved the problem of the standing and destiny of the Old Israel, but it secured a hope of resurrection unto eternal life to all who believe in Christ; whether Jews or Gentiles originally, they are now the heirs of the promise.

As a Jew, Paul was bound to regard predestination and election as basic ideas. Prior to everything and in

* *Paul: The Theology of the Apostle in the Light of Jewish Religious History*, trans. by H. Knight (1961), p. 234.

everything is the will and purpose of God. He reveals it in history to His servants. It is directed to the great consummation in which God is all in all and the elect are with Him for ever.

Who are the elect? Not Israel the nation but the children of Abraham whose distinguishing mark is faith. But now that Christ has died and risen this means all who believe in Christ; the Church is the true Israel of God.

Paul's typological form of thought gives priority to the notions of representation and heritage. All men are in Adam by birth. All the faithful are in Abraham. All the elect are in Christ, the seed of Abraham and the Second Adam. From this it is but a step, though a very individual one, to what has been called Paul's "Christ-Mysticism". Not only are the elect in Christ but Christ is in them. All that is true of the one is true of the other and what has happened to the one is happening and will happen to the other. Thus the death and resurrection of Christ are the pattern of the Christian's life. But the union of the Christian with Christ is so constitutive of his existence as a Christian that he is even now a man who has died and risen again as Christ has.

Paul therefore at one and the same time looks for the resurrection as an eschatological event and regards the Christian as now risen with Christ. It is as if his present experience and convictions overlap the interval in which it is still not true that the new age is fully come, and proleptically as well as representationally secure for him now the blessings of the age to come.

How is this proleptic present experience related to the eschatological expectation? Are we justified in taking Paul's own experience and the way in which it was comprehended by him as normative for Christian life and thought?

Even if it is possible to see how his very act of believing in Christ as risen Messiah irrupted into the familiar plan of the last things and required its own expression as the actual situation of a man "in Christ", it is not easy to harmonise the "mystical" with the eschatological so as to yield a consistent doctrine of Christian resurrection. Is it a state of being or a hope for the future? In Paul it is both, but how long can the two be held side by side? And what conception of resurrection does each imply?

The expectation of an event is well represented in the New Testament as the primary form while the Fourth Gospel more than any other non-Pauline writing gives prominence to the "mystical" aspect. It can portray Jesus as saying that the believer has passed already from death to life and can merge the Parousia with the gift of the Holy Spirit.

The co-existence of these twin conceptions depends on the survival of belief in the eschatological programme on the one hand and the continued availability of Paul's expression of his own Christian experience as a valid doctrine of the Christian life on the other. If belief in the eschatological programme should fail or be modified, if the Christian experience should no longer find its adequate expression in terms appropriate to the experience of Paul, then the difficulties inherent in the co-existence of a "mystical" with an eschatological doctrine of resurrection will become intolerable. The post-Pauline literature in the New Testament shows that no lasting equilibrium was possible though both continued to find a place in the theology of the Church.

To this day the devotional literature of the Church is more indebted to the thought of union with Christ, drawing sustenance from the "Christ in you" teaching of Paul and from the "mystical" element in the Fourth Gospel, while its doctrinal literature holds on tenaciously to an attenuated form of the eschatological hope.

Note on the Pauline Corpus

For some time past it has been assumed that we can never be sure how many of the 14 letters attributed to him were actually written by Paul. The effect of this assumption has been that most scholars exclude Hebrews and the Pastorals and regard the remaining ten as material from which the theology of Paul may be gathered.

The difficulty of subsuming the whole range of thought and style in these letters has been overcome by endowing Paul with these capabilities, and the mind of Paul is that which is revealed in these letters. The circularity of argument involved in this situation is obvious.

Some years ago Dr. W. C. Wake published in the *Journal of the Royal Statistical Society* (Series A, Volume 120) an objective test for homogeneous authorship, based on sentence length. His conclusion was that Romans, Galatians, 1 Corinthians and 2 Corinthians 10–13 were homogeneous. The other Epistles were the work of more than one hand distinct from the first four.

More recently the work of A. Q. Morton on the same principles has confirmed the general conclusion, particularly in his paper in the Festschrift for Prof. G. H. C. Macgregor, *The Authorship of the Pauline Corpus*. In it he studies the occurrences of "kai" in all homogeneous Greek prose, and finds consistency in the first four epistles only.

This kind of argument is new and therefore uncongenial to many, but in time it will be seen to be unanswerable and will lead to a re-assessment of Paul and his theology.

CHAPTER TEN

ENCOUNTERING A PARADOX

THE interim which was not foreseen, the hiatus between the resurrection of Christ and the overt continuation of the eschatological programme, created two major problems. In the first place, this unpredicted period had to find a place within the plan of God since it could not be left as an enigma outside the purpose and foreknowledge of God. As we have seen, it provides the special revelation and prerogative of Paul as the Apostle to the Gentiles. It is consecrated to the greater glory of God in extending His mercy to those outside the original promise and covenant of Israel.

The second major problem arises in relation to the nature and prospects of those who now believe. No provision is made within the general eschatological scheme for the situation in which they now find themselves. Such a situation was not foreseen. They are no longer of the old age; they belong to the new. But the new is not fully come. What are they and what is in store for them?

Pauline theology is a vast subject and we must not be drawn into its fascinating mazes. Our particular interest is in the place and significance of resurrection in the Pauline Epistles. What questions are raised by the fact that believers have hopes which are not yet fulfilled? What is their present standing and what will be their future state? What is the position of the Christian man in the interim between believing in Christ and being made perfect in Christ? This is the new kind of question raised by the fact that Christ has been manifested, but the eschatological programme seems to be temporarily in abeyance.

Paul regards the Christian man as one who has received new status and new prospects but is nonetheless compelled to live in circumstances which belong to his old status and his old prospects. The Christian, while still in this world, is being fitted for another world. At the same time the new status and indeed the other world are real and present in some measure by instalment. The Christian man is a paradox within a paradox.

Many of the difficulties in the Pauline writings arise from this ambiguous situation. Paul is addressing himself to men and to circumstances in an age in which both are unresolved complexes of a transition which is meantime arrested. He speaks to them now as "saints", now as "carnal men". He visualises their environment now as "this world", now as "the world to come". This is the inevitable predicament of the interim period.

In such a situation systematic theology is not possible. It can be achieved only at the expense of ignoring the essence of the paradox. Paul is constrained by his conception of the time in which he lives to ask and answer questions that had not been conceivable before. It is not surprising that some of his answers were *ad hoc* and consistency far to seek.

If we ask what has happened to the man who believes that Jesus has been raised from the dead, the answer is that he is a "new creature"—but not completely. He is being prepared for the life to come but is still required to live this life. He has received something from God which is supernatural. It certifies his right to a place in the consummation. In the resurrection he will have part. It is his destiny to reign with Christ. At the judgment he will not be condemned. But unless the programme moves forward he will die as other men do. Some already have. The consequence is problems of a practical and pastoral nature which strain the framework of Paul's theology.

Why do those who belong to Christ die? This is obviously a burning question and the bewilderment it creates is due simply to the fact that death is not congruous with the expectations of those who believe. And death here is not spiritual, but physical. Why should a man who has spiritually passed from death, judgment and all the consequences of unbelief, be subject to physical death? This is unexpected. It is a consequence of the interim.

What is more is that it could be thought that those who have died in the faith may thereby have missed something of the reward of everlasting life. Entry into this believing state initially must have been conceived as dispensing with the necessity of death for those living in the era following the resurrection of Christ. Otherwise it is hard to understand the grave concern with which Paul treats the matter. His impassioned insistence that the dead have not missed any of the glory to come if they are believers emphasises that here he undertakes an emergency operation. This is not a situation which has been foreseen. There is no provision for it in the general eschatological timetable. He must improvise, even if in a masterly fashion.

But if death, physical death, is something to be anticipated by some Christians after all, what is the condition of the dead in Christ and what their prospects? They are asleep in Jesus and they will be awaked when the next stage takes place. Then they and the living shall leave behind the world of sin and death and be for ever with Christ.

That the living will not pass through death at the

consummation involves the idea that some transformation is going on within the believer which will make resurrection unnecessary should the programme move to its climax during their lifetime. The believer is in process of becoming, or proleptically is, a new creature, fit for glory, and this process will be completed instanter at the coming of Christ. Since Paul believes that flesh and blood cannot enter the kingdom of God, yet those who do are clothed in a body of glory, there is much room for miracle.

The ambiguity introduced into the situation by this time-lag is seen in the doctrine of baptism (cf. Rom. 6). It is by baptism that a believing man enters the body of those who are "in Christ". Paul does not think it is important to be a baptiser (1 Cor. 1:3–17) but it is important to be baptised, for thereby one is identified with Christ.

But this identification has a double reference. The baptised not only enjoys and inherits the benefit of all that Christ has done and will do for him. Baptism guarantees that all that is done in the person of Christ for him is genuinely recapitulated in his own person.

Thus, as Christ died, the baptised are dead (to sin) and must die daily, till the next stage is come. As He was raised so they (now) are raised to newness of life and must themselves be raised at a future date. The daily dying is not bound to end in a final death (some will be alive at His coming), but the resurrection is re-enacted for all in present experience and will be objectively re-enacted at the Parousia, except, that is, as "transformation" for those still alive at His coming. Here the boundaries between fact and metaphor, faith and knowledge, experience and history have all collapsed.

It is the Christian's position in time—i.e. between the Resurrection and the Parousia—which necessitates this ambivalence in thought and expression in relation to baptism, death and resurrection. This interim is not, of course, a vacuum. It has, as we have seen, its own place and purpose in the unfolding plan and Christians have now the knowledge of forgiveness, the presence of Christ in them as the hope of glory, the arrabon or advance "as a security that the whole will be paid afterwards" (Souter). But the tension of living in this interim points up the divine discontent of primitive Christianity and puts a premium on yearning and hope and consequently on endeavour.

One of the most important passages in the New Testament as far as our subject is concerned is the fifteenth of 1 Corinthians. Its importance arises from two causes— this is the only passage in which a New Testament writer gives detailed account of the process of eschatological resurrection with special reference to the mode of resurrection: it is also the passage which most clearly indicates the influence of the Hellenistic doctrine of immortality on the traditional doctrine of resurrection. This latter does not necessarily imply deliberate Hellenism on Paul's part; it rather indicates how far Hellenistic thought has become naturalised in the Jewish conception of last things.

The accepted principle of racial and religious solidarity is basic to Paul's interpretation of the Christian's status. Adam is the racial head and representative and what is true of him is true of all his descendants. Christ is the new Adam and what is true of Him is true of His spiritual descendants.

Since Christ died, believers are "dead to sin". (This is obviously conventional reasoning since the death of Christ was physical and He is not conceived of as having been "alive to sin" in the sense in which Adam's sons all are.)

Since He has been raised, all believers are raised in present union with Christ or will be raised at the Parousia. (Again the reasoning is conventional since, if the resurrection of Jesus is conceived as physical, the consequences are not necessarily so for the believer since those alive at His coming need no resurrection.)

The argument is tenable only if spiritual and physical death are interchangeable and Paul, apparently, found no difficulty here. But it is clear that the argument is contained within the context of the eschatological idea. It is not effective as argument since there is no definition of terms such as is necessary to establish consequences and conclusion. A scriptural idea has been shaped to support an independent thesis, namely, that since Christ is raised believers are certain of entering the resurrection life whether they live or die.

The passage makes three definite statements about the Corinthians. These are valuable because they help us to see something of the other side of the argument. Since we have no other literature on the controversy, we are under the handicap of having to deduce from the statement on the one side what positions are being maintained by the other, without the assurance that they are not misstated and without the benefit of knowing by what arguments these positions are being supported.

These three statements are (1) that the Corinthians received the Gospel, (2) that some say there is no resurrection and (3) that a practice of baptism for the dead is in vogue at Corinth.

(1) Paul's summary of the Gospel which the Corinthians received (vv. 3–8) is that Christ died, was buried, was raised. These are the articles of belief which Paul transmitted. There is no reference to the Parousia, but the same is true of other future events which were un-

doubtedly matters of expectation. When Paul speaks of "His coming" (v. 23) it is as of something known and not needing special definition.

It may be that 1 Corinthians contains the first written reference to the Parousia in a homogeneous document by an identifiable author. If so, it is evidence that the Parousia expectation lies deep in the earliest days of the Church. It is beyond dispute that belief in the resurrection of Jesus is there at the beginning and this belief requires His presence in power for its completion.

(2) That being so, the fact that some in Corinth in some sense deny the resurrection is disconcerting. The extent to which and the setting in which resurrection is denied are not easy to discover from a passage written to confute the denial.

The Corinthian Church is rent into parties on various grounds apart from this question. These grounds are apparently doctrinal as well as ethical, questions of belief and of loyalty to teachers as well as questions of morals. Paul is not dealing with a Church which has split so much as with splinter groups. The question of the resurrection is dealt with at length, presumably as one which threatens a radical departure from the essentials of Christianity.

What is the nature of this threat? There are three possibilities: (a) a denial of the resurrection of Jesus, (b) a disagreement as to the mode of entry into eternal life and (c) a denial of the resurrection of believers. This last could be based on an argument that believers are already risen with Christ, a position maintained and expounded by Paul in Romans.

Paul refers in his letters to all three of these positions. He insists on the actuality of the resurrection of Christ. He devotes a section to the mode of resurrection. He

refers to the non-necessity of resurrection for those believers (the majority) who are still alive at the Parousia.

We are therefore required to ask what would be regarded as a denial of the resurrection in the eyes of Paul
and what was possible in the situation at Corinth. Both
are difficult questions. Obviously (a) an outright denial
of the resurrection of Jesus would qualify; but since this
is the distinctive mark of a church it is unlikely that this
was the situation. As regards (c) Paul is willing to con-
cede that some believers would not require eschatological
resurrection; they would be "changed". There is no
direct clash here.

It would seem, therefore, that the most likely point of
controversy is (b) the mode of entry into eternal life. A
disagreement on this could be interpreted as both an outright denial of the possibility of resurrection and as denial
of the resurrection of believers and so subsume all three
possibilities.

If the Corinthians were unwilling to accept the doctrine
of bodily resurrection of believers, this is not necessarily
a denial that Jesus is Lord, nor is it a repudiation of the
hope of the life to come. But it could be represented as
such by one to whom bodily resurrection in some form is
essential to the belief in the Lordship of Jesus and to the
reality of the life to come.

It is easy to understand that those who come to Christianity out of a culture which accepts the immortality of
the soul might object to a Jewish conception of bodily
resurrection, which they might even mistakenly regard
as having nothing to add to their real expectations and
whose form appeared crude and uncongenial.

We know too little about what a primitive Gentile
Church was like to make any dogmatic statements about
what could or could not have been believed in one church

in particular, when as yet the notion of orthodoxy is still to be fashioned. Contrast the position in which Justin (martyred *c.* 165) could speak of those who say "there is no resurrection of the dead, but as soon as we die, our souls are taken up to heaven" and brand them unhesitatingly as unorthodox, for "I and all other Christians of orthodox belief know that there will be a resurrection of the flesh and also a millennium in Jerusalem" (Dialogue 80).

(3) On the vexed question of baptism for the dead, it would appear that even those who believed in a blessed life beyond the grave apart from the body, might use such a ceremony on behalf of their dead. Provided there is a possibility of a wretched as well as a happy immortality, the question as to whether this is "bodily" or not is not crucial to the ceremony. It is enough that it has reference to and in some way is thought to guarantee a blessed future life.

The question of whether the refusal to accept the idea of bodily resurrection was carried back by its protagonists to the resurrection of Jesus is one on which we have no evidence. But it is theoretically possible that some could believe in Christ as Lord without feeling the obligation to believe that the same body rose from the tomb. Indeed, the argument of Paul in the rest of the chapter would seem to support such a position insofar as it differentiates the corruptible from the incorruptible.

It might seem to some of the Corinthians that Paul denies their position but appears to maintain his own by rhetorical sleight of hand. He agrees that "the" body is not resurrected but insists that "a" body must be resurrected.

One of the main interests of the chapter, indeed, resides in the answer to the question: How are the dead raised? This question also derives its urgency from the particular paradoxical situation created by the unforeseen interim.

The conventional treatments of the subject do not have to cope with an interval of apparent divine inactivity. The New Age is most generally conceived as being ushered in dramatically and with impressive suddenness. There is no gap between the word and the deed of God. Paul retains this aspect in the conception of the next stage when the hiatus is over. It will happen in the twinkling of an eye.

But the present pause provokes questions not envisaged heretofore, questions which become urgent the more certain believers are that the time is near and the more opportunity there is in the Gentile Churches for a conflict of Greek and Hebrew conceptions of the life to come. The survival of the soul requires no such urgency and creates no such perplexity, because here the dead are not raised and those who have died may now be enjoying immortality.

Paul cannot relinquish the bodily resurrection idea in spite of the difficulties. He must therefore attempt to prefigure the process as well as the time of resurrection. In so doing he meets the inevitable limitations of logic in relation to a matter which is essentially one of conviction. It is a situation where the best that can be said is, "I do not know: I believe" and whatever goes beyond that is inadequate.

Paul, however, requires to go beyond that, because one man's conviction is not sufficient if another man is asking an explanation. Some independent support must be offered beyond the bare assertion.

The "mystery" that not all shall die but all shall be changed (vv. 51, 52) is evidently new material to the Corinthians and may be an original contribution to the

things that belong to the end. It stands at the borderline
of the two conceptions of Messiah's kingdom, the earthly
reign and the kingdom of glory. Paul evidently believes
that the saints enter a glorious kingdom with a body of
glory when Christ's reign is established *de facto*. But
whether this would be accepted by Paul's opponents as
authoritative prophecy would depend, of course, on their
general disposition towards him.

Paul turns to the analogy of the seed. But it is no more
than a likening of one process to another, based on the
succession of one condition to another. It is no explanation of either process. Neither the principle of the continuity of life here with life hereafter nor the nature of the
resurrection body emerges from this passage. If what is
sown is not what is raised, wherein lies the association?
If it is, is death but the death of the body and can the
separable soul not survive alone? If by that which is
sown in weakness is meant not physical death but the
meagre beginnings of the Christian's life here and now
as resurrection life in embryo as it were, does this also die
to be recreated at the resurrection?

Such precise questions do not belong to the age of
Paul. But they show that for him the mode of resurrection is something which he can approach only from
within the eschatological frame of reference. They show
also that resurrection and immortality ideas are both
present to him, but the latter must serve the former if
they are to have any place within his thought. Ultimately
resurrection for Paul is an act of God and is not to
be explained but experienced and scarcely to be described.

The quest for consistency here is vain. Those who
feel that it is essential, transpose the whole matter to a
mystical or metaphysical key. They believe that what Paul

said must be authoritative for Christian belief ever after and cannot therefore be subject to incongruity.

That considerable philosophical and theological systems can be raised on the basis of Paul's letters is granted. Because the apostle stood at a crux in religious development and wrestled with hitherto unformulated questions, his letters are fitted for continued reinterpretation.

But all speculation on Pauline theology which fails to recognise the limits imposed by his general conception of history and prophecy are scarcely to be called Pauline theology themselves. And to constrain his thought into a detailed systematic pattern instead of recognising it as an existential attempt to grapple with the needs of his own age in terms of his own eschatological preconceptions, is to evacuate the letters of life and interest.

It is fairer to Paul and to the temporary purpose of his letters to accept his own premises and admit the incongruities. His stature is not thereby diminished. We ought not to blame him for not being born in the 20th century. Essentially he regards resurrection as a divine miracle which results in fitness to live and reign with Christ. How it happens is ultimately God's own secret, but that it happens is an assurance which belongs to all who are "in Christ".

CHAPTER ELEVEN

GOSPEL ASSUMPTIONS

ALL six major books of the New Testament are composite in their structure. They have been compiled, not composed by a single author.

This has long been recognised regarding the Synoptic Gospels and Acts. Many have seen in the Apocalypse a reissue with additions and modifications of a Jewish tract. Few scholars would regard it as the spontaneous production of one man.

Till recently, however, the Fourth Gospel has been regarded by many as a unity, even when there has been no agreement as to authorship. From now on account will have to be taken of the work of Macgregor and Morton. In *The Structure of the Fourth Gospel* (Oliver & Boyd, 1961) the case for the interlocking of two main distinguishable sources is made out.

This thesis explains certain puzzling features in the construction of the Fourth Gospel and cannot be dismissed simply because its statistical technique is unfamiliar. Its importance lies in the fact that it is the first time that genuinely objective criteria have been used in the solution of a textual problem in the New Testament.

Since none of the Gospels as they stand can be regarded as an original document, the difficulty of arriving at trustworthy historical material must be recognised. It should not be exaggerated, but neither must it be minimised. But the reasons for which the Church originally included those books in its canon cannot appear so cogent to us today. We are no longer able to believe that they were written by apostles or composed by apostolic men. They were made by selection and redaction.

That they contain early and trustworthy material is not to be doubted, but this can be discovered and established only through the application of historical method. The day is long past when it was possible to quote a text beginning, "Jesus said", with the certainty that it is a word of the historic Jesus. This applies to the Synoptic Gospels as well as to the Fourth. The days of rule-of-thumb methods are past. If Christianity depended on inerrancy in Gospel tradition then its prospects would be dim indeed.

Recent scholarship seems to have established that the purpose of the Gospels is not biography or history, but "*kerugma*" and "*didache*". This is very natural. It does not lead to the conclusion that there is no history in the Gospels, but it does mean that history is not their primary interest and that history is always in danger of being used to serve that primary interest.

There seems little doubt that this in fact has happened in some instances. It is at least worth asking, for example, whether in Matthew the infant Jesus was taken to Egypt in order that He might be called out of Egypt in terms of prophecy.

It would be a safe proceeding to be on guard against this kind of modification in the record when the subject is directly related to the primary interest of the Gospels. On the other hand, when no dogmatic purpose is to be served, the chances are that no such modification is likely to be introduced.

The only writer in the New Testament who has a sense of biography akin to that of Plutarch, for example, and a sense of history akin to that of Thucydides, for instance, is the compiler of Luke–Acts. Even so, it is very far from meeting the requirements of the modern historiographer. For this we cannot blame the first-century writers. But neither can we be content not to ask questions of the kind which never occurred to these writers, not to apply standards of precision of which they were unaware.

It is surely a grave disservice to truth and to Christianity to continue to take the Gospels more or less as they stand, when we are conscious that their nature and purpose makes this illegitimate from the historical point of view. It is as false to make Genesis preach the doctrine of evolution, as it is to use the Johannine text, "that they may be one", as a conclusive argument for the union of Churches in the mid-twentieth century. Historical investigation is the only safeguard against using scripture as a book of all-purpose golden texts.

When we approach the Gospels regarding the doctrine of resurrection, we are involved in a subject which was of supreme dogmatic interest to the writers. We should expect to find that Christian belief up to the time of their compilation will be reflected in their pages. We should not be surprised if history is sometimes unable to establish its priority on ground subsequently overrun by dogma.

This will be particularly liable to happen in regard to the central tenet of the faith—the resurrection of Jesus the Messiah. It will not surprise us to find that this tenet of faith conceived as event is foretold by Jesus in the Gospels and believed to have been previously forecast in Scripture, even if such considerations ill accord with the general tenor of other events recounted by the same writers.

Messiahship and Resurrection, the twin pillars of the initial faith of the Church, have become increasingly difficult to trace back into the pre-crucifixion era as having been appropriated by Jesus to Himself in the days of His flesh. The two belong together in the earliest stratum of the Church's preaching; they made the Church. But to establish them as fact or prophecy directly related to Jesus in the pre-crucifixion period has become an onerous undertaking.

The matter of Messiahship was brought prominently to the fore by Wrede and Schweitzer at the beginning of the century in their attempts to explain or to justify the structure of Mark's Gospel and the chronological sequence of Jesus' career. "The inconsistency between the public life of Jesus and His Messianic claim lies either in the nature of the Jewish Messianic conception or in the representation of the Evangelist."*

Schweitzer chose the former alternative, Wrede the latter. In the *Quest* Schweitzer maintained that Jesus thought of Himself as Messiah in the terms current in His own day and regarded Himself as *Christus futurus*. Wrede, on the other hand, argued that the only explanation of the incongruities in Mark regarding Messiahship is that Mark carried back the title applied to Jesus in the Church into the period of the earthly ministry of Jesus and that this was unhistorical.

Schweitzer's resulting portrait of the historical Jesus has not been acceptable; but the alternative is drastic. Nevertheless, scholars of the calibre of Loisy, Guignebert, Dibelius and Bultmann have felt bound to accept it, either in the form of an unconfessed Messiahship or in the form of a denial that Jesus claimed to be or was Messiah.†

* Schweitzer, *The Quest of the Historical Jesus*, p. 335.

† See e.g. quotation on p. 101; also Gunther Bornkamm, *Jesus of Nazareth*, Appendix iii. "The Messianic Titles in Jesus' References to Himself".

In any case, the difficulties of maintaining that Jesus laid claim to the title have certainly not diminished in the last half century and the probability that Wrede was fundamentally right is consequently greater.

At the same time and for different reasons it has become less easy to maintain that Jesus precisely forecast His own resurrection. A quotation from F. C. Grant will show the present position. He is commenting on the first of the three predictions of death and resurrection in Mark's Gospel (8:31; 9:31; 10:34).

"That Jesus realised the dangers surrounding him, and recognized the hazard he took in going to Jerusalem, is certainly most probable: but that he predicted the detailed events that were to occur there is difficult to believe. For one thing, the disciples were not in the least impressed by the three predictions; they behaved throughout the Passion as if they had never heard these words. For another, the attitude of Jesus himself does not bear out this detailed provision of the circumstances. Finally, the quality of his martyr death is neutralized, and his heroism is made unreal and reduced to the mere histrionic performance of an assigned role, if he foresaw in advance the full details of the passion and the eventual denouement of his career. It is chiefly for these reasons that scholars now view the three announcements as 'secondary', i.e. as either composed by Mark to suit his dramatic-theological purpose, or at least modified to suit the passion narrative."*

The close relationship of these two questions—Messiahship and Resurrection—as constituting major problems within the Gospel record of the ministry of Jesus has not always been clearly recognised, but they are inseparably linked and the quest for the historical Jesus must come to grips with the alternatives that are available.

* F. C. Grant in *The Interpreter's Bible*, Vol. 7, pp. 767, 768.

Perhaps the interest over the past 25 years in the "Messianic consciousness", "realised eschatology" and "the second advent" is best understood in the light of the Schweitzer–Wrede dilemma, as well as the flight from historical criticism which has been so evident in other quarters.

At all events, the possibility of establishing a historical foundation for a life of Jesus is still far from agreed. There is certainly no consensus of opinion as to how far the Gospels in their eschatological content, and particularly in reference to the words of Jesus, are subject to misrepresentation or intrusion. They are not free from the kind of pressure due to the fact that they are written in the light of a faith which required to be substantiated at as early a date in the life of Jesus as possible.

Although those who compiled and recounted resurrection narratives such as appear in the Gospels believed they were dealing with a historical event, historical criticism cannot substantiate such an event. Every New Testament reference to the resurrection of Jesus arises from a conviction which correlates Jesus' Messiahship and the current doctrine of resurrection. Resurrection regarded as event is a derivative of resurrection as a dogmatic postulate. The idea that the content of "belief in resurrection" is an event in past history makes nonsense of the Christian faith: that it includes an event as distinct from belief in event is not capable of historical proof. This aspect of the problem is dealt with in the next section of this book.

From the Synoptic Gospels it is impossible not to conclude that the teaching of Jesus, in proportion as it touched on the subject of resurrection, is no different from that which we have seen to have been current in the age in which He lived. It would appear that the underlying assumptions of all resurrection references on the lips of Jesus in the Synoptics are precisely those of which we have more detailed knowledge in the Apocalyptic literature which we have already surveyed. The teaching is no more precise. It offers no special revelation.

It is assumed to be the common belief of the times, except among the Sadducees, whose distinctive tenets arose in the inter-Testamental period as the result of a conservative attitude to Scripture and a worldly-wise attitude to politics. They found no resurrection in the Pentateuch and were doubtless sophisticated enough to regard the immortality of the soul as a more likely possibility than the gross resurrection of the body, when the Scripture they cherished as inspired left them free to choose.

The fact that the teaching of Jesus adds nothing to the doctrine of resurrection might be regarded as disquieting, especially since this doctrine was to become so central to the Christian faith. But any attempt to find in the Synoptic Gospels some new and original development of thought on this subject seems to be fruitless. Nothing which cannot be paralleled in the known literature of the era is present. The entire programme of last things is taken for granted.

This is one more indication of the way in which the New Testament achieved its distinctive quality. As we have already noted, that quality is due not to the teaching of Jesus but to the faith about Jesus. In so far as we are able to go beyond that faith into the pre-crucifixion period, we find nothing which is not indigenous to the period in terms of doctrine. It is the life and work of Jesus—what we today would call the personality—that receives priority here.

It is the life and work of Jesus which Mark records

as the signal event of Messiahship. The words of Jesus are important only as the words of the Messiah. Even in Matthew, where more of the teaching is preserved, it is obvious that the reason why it is to be cherished is not because it is new, but because Messiah's lips distil the wisdom of the ages. Nowhere do the Synoptists expect men to be convinced that Jesus is Messiah because of what He says. They expect His teaching to be accepted because He is Messiah, not because it is new, however they may wonder at it.

As far as we can ascertain, the expectation of Jesus regarding resurrection in general is unexceptional. The survivors of the final generation, along with the righteous dead who will be raised to life again, will receive eternal life in a Kingdom which will have no end. The wicked will have been condemned and cast out of God's presence.

There is no teaching as to the mode of transformation from the present to the life to come, such as we have noted in the Pauline letters. This problem is not predominant, though references to "this generation" and the adaption of parables to the needs of a later age show that there is a general sense of urgency and expectancy. It is not "how" but "when" are the dead raised, that is the question.

That the Synoptic Gospels show no trace of the modifications to resurrection teaching introduced by Paul to meet the exigencies of his particular situation, is worthy of note. It may mean that, while the tradition behind the Synoptic Gospels was one which could not be guaranteed not to misinterpret the teaching of Jesus, it was also one which was incapable of deliberate addition and invention.

But it may also mean that, while the Pauline teaching on the subject of resurrection was destined to become that

of the Church, it was at first a personal and isolated interpretation of the course of events and was not readily acceptable to the Palestinian or Jewish section of the Church.
By the time the Pauline Corpus was accepted, the element of extreme urgency had been refined and the time
was ripe for some consolidation of Christian thought.

The Fourth Gospel presents its own interest in this as
in other matters. Eschatology here, on the whole, is no
longer crude and urgent. The focus of attention has
moved from the return of Christ to the resurrection life as
begun now through faith, although the more primitive
eschatology is still represented.

Those who have seen the Fourth Gospel as standing
in the Pauline tradition are to some extent justified. The
New Age is not only begun, but the process which Paul
thought to be temporarily arrested is in fact proceeding.
Eternal life is not a gift which is eschatologically conferred but a present experience through faith in the Son
of God.

This is a continuation of the Pauline thought that believers are now being made fit for the life of the New Age.
But the eschatological event to which he looked forward
has been taken out of the foreground of vision. The
emphasis is more deliberately upon present union with
Christ. He does not guarantee, He is, the resurrection
and the life. To believe in Him is to have passed from
death to life. The event of resurrection is not its own
significance. The event is the flesh of which the word is
the reality. Lazarus is raised but not to prove that resurrection is possible. The miracle shows that Christ is the
resurrection and that to believe in Him is to live.

Of this Gospel it is much more difficult to say that
addition and invention are not possible. The Jesus who
speaks is not the historical Jesus but the risen Lord. But

what guarantee can be offered that these are the words of the risen Lord?

The teaching of Jesus in the Fourth Gospel may be a possible development of the Gospel which the Jesus of the Synoptics proclaimed and embodied. But it is dangerous to confuse history and prophecy and it often results in sanctifying what has taken place. It is: therefore it is true.

Because the Fourth Gospel exists, it has *ipso facto* tended to be regarded as the final and most spiritual exposition of the life and teaching of Jesus—if not of what He said and did, then of what He meant. This is a very precarious situation. Nothing can absolve us from the necessity to attempt to decide how far it can be accepted as history and how far as inspired Christian speculation.

The "mother-nurture" of the Gospel of St. John may be Essenic and the way of thought and literary style in some parts are significantly close to what may be found in the Qumran texts. Nevertheless the final form of the Gospel and the function it performed in the development of Christian theology are related to the transition from an eschatological to a mystical and devotional emphasis. Both are present in different parts of the Gospel, but it cannot be doubted that the eschatological is the original setting of the life and teaching of Jesus and of the first generation of his followers.

PART III

THE RESURRECTION NARRATIVES

CHAPTER TWELVE

THE CRUCIAL INTERVAL

IT may be said that the birth of Christianity is hidden in the tomb of Jesus. When the tomb was no longer significant to Jesus' disciples, Christianity was already born; but so long as their hearts were with Jesus in death, they could not be aware of His presence in life. They were therefore unable to say the things which were later to make disciples in addition to their own number. The birth of Christianity took place when some person or some company of persons turned away (metaphorically) from the tomb, saying, "He is not here: He is risen."

It is true that the tomb once again became significant but in a quite different way—when "He is risen" became, "He was raised". That this is not simply a quibble about a form of words can be seen if we reflect on certain facts which belong to the nature of temporal awareness. The experience of the first person to realise that Jesus is not dead is not the same thing as the belief by subsequent persons that He was raised from the dead. The initial experience is creative; the later experiences may be only confirmatory or imitative. Further, to the subsequent experient the initial experience has become history.

This is not to deny that all who believe that Jesus is alive share something in common which entitles them all to be called Christians. But there is a unique quality belonging to the first affirmation of such a faith as far as Christianity regarded as a movement is concerned. It may mean that the first affirmation becomes history in a sense which all following affirmations can never bear.

The subsequent story confirms this in various ways. There is evidence that those who were of the original group when the first affirmation was made had a unique place in the Church, principally Peter. Even in the 2nd century, a teacher who had had contact with one believed to have been of that select company was specially revered. When the Church was fighting heresy it relied upon the words and deeds of those who were there when everything began.

Again, the second generation of believers (even the first generation, apart from those later called apostles) experience the benefits of Christian fellowship, but depend on the word of the apostles for the assurance that Christ is risen. There is no evidence that every new believer had his own specially repeated revelation of the Risen Christ, although he did enjoy the blessings that flowed from believing in the Risen Christ. In the first instance he believed the word, the report, the witness of the apostles (or of others concerning them) that Jesus is risen. His life was a Christian experience in the present. His faith, i.e. what he believed, was a received tradition. He believed on authority and that belief was essential to the Christian experience.

There is no ground for suggesting that early Christians each enjoyed their own personal experience which convinced them that Jesus is alive. The evidence is that they believed and found thereby the Christian experience. In theological terms, as the New Testament insists, faith precedes salvation.

The message to outsiders was to the effect that Jesus is alive on the testimony of a few and that He is concerned in a specific way with the destiny of every soul. Where possible, this message is reinforced from the Old Testament Scriptures. It is not therefore a direct revelation to everyone who is to become a Christian, but in the first instance a proposition to be supported by witnesses and testimony. The experience of being a Christian is direct, but the creed of the Christian is communicated. It is therefore historical and capable of being traced to its first moments.

But this particular analytical interest in its beginnings is not to be expected initially. It appears only after the apostolic age has almost gone. Even then it is not the kind of interest that we now take; and it has been satisfied by concrete stories in which the principal characters take part and the empty tomb is regarded as a further proof that Jesus was raised from the dead, in addition to the witness of the apostles and the testimony of Old Testament Scripture.

This interest in the tomb after Christianity has been in existence for some time is quite different from the interest of the first disciples on the morrow of the crucifixion. Once the certainty arises that He is risen, the tomb is of no consequence to the disciples except as a symbol of death having been destroyed. There is no reason to suppose that any early Christian ever made a pilgrimage to the tomb of Christ.

The reason why we must begin at the tomb is simply because this is the latest point at which we are safe to say, "Up to now, Christianity does not exist." We shall need to go back beyond this in our investigation. But this is the *terminus a quo* for the crucial interval in which it can be said that Christianity was born. The *terminus ad quem* is not so readily fixed.

The question therefore confronts us: What is the interval between the burial of Jesus and the objective certainty that the Church is in existence? We are not yet concerned to ask what was the course of events between, e.g. the crucifixion and the Day of Pentecost. We simply ask: How long was it before the assurance which created the Church came into being? It might seem that this is a very limited and trivial subject of investigation and, in any case, it may be thought quite impossible to reach a conclusion. But it can be pointed out that unless we know the interval we cannot begin to study what happened in it and, secondly, that the paucity or doubtful validity of the materials at hand for answering such a question is no greater an obstacle than it is in some other inquiries. Scholars still debate about the day on which Jesus was crucified and the precise course of events on that day. The fact is, the immediate post-crucifixion days are an epoch-making period of time whose duration is of great consequence. Nothing prevents us from examining what evidence there is and using the same kind of historical method here as elsewhere. Our interest requires us to do so.

Our first duty, then, is to survey all the material on the subject, irrespective of its provenance, and discover whether there is any unanimity on the question. If not, we must inquire whether there is any explanation of the disparity which would lead to probability. This is conventional practice.

Since we are concerned at present only with the evidence of the time lapse between the crucifixion and the first sign of the distinctive Christian belief, it will be sufficient to summarise the data simply in the order in which the books appear in the New Testament.

Matthew:

Mary Magdalene and the other Mary go to the sepulchre towards dawn on the first day of the week. An angel

shows the empty tomb, proclaims Jesus risen and instructs them to tell His disciples He will meet them in
Galilee. The women meet Jesus Himself on the way
back. He greets them and they hold His feet and worship
Him. He repeats the instructions just given. (28:1–10)

In Galilee the eleven disciples meet Jesus as pre-
arranged. They worship Him "but some doubted". He
commissions them and promises His constant presence.
(28:16–20)

Mark:

Mary Magdalene, Mary the mother of Jesus and
Salome go to the tomb early on the first day of the week.
The stone has been moved. An angel tells them Jesus is
risen and instructs them to tell His disciples "and Peter"
He will meet them in Galilee. The women depart hastily
and say nothing of what had taken place. (16:1–8)

Luke:

Women go to the tomb early on the first day of the
week. The stone has been moved. Two angels remind
them Jesus said He would be crucified and rise the third
day. They return and tell the disciples. Some don't
believe. (23:55–24:12)

The same day "two of them" go to Emmaus. A
stranger joins them and instructs them on the scriptural
necessity of Christ's death and resurrection. Only later
do they realise the stranger was Jesus. They hurry back
to Jerusalem with the news. In the meantime the disciples have heard that Jesus has appeared to Peter.
(24:13–35)

There and then He appears to them all, convincing
them by showing His hands and feet and eating in their
presence. He instructs them on the scriptural necessity

of His death and resurrection and commissions them. He orders them to stay in Jerusalem till they are clothed with power. He leads them to Bethany, blesses them and departs. (24:36–52)

John:

Mary goes to the tomb early on the first day of the week. The stone has been moved. She goes and tells Peter and the "other". They run to the tomb. Peter enters followed by the "other" (who believes) and finds the tomb empty. They return to their homes. (20:1–10)

Mary weeps outside the tomb, speaks to the gardener who is revealed as Jesus. He warns her not to touch Him, tells of His imminent ascension and instructs her to inform "my brethren", which she does. (20:11–18)

The same evening Jesus comes through closed doors to His disciples, blesses them, shows His hands and side. They rejoice, receive another blessing and are commissioned. He breathes on them, they receive the Holy Spirit and the power to forgive and retain sins. The appearance is repeated for Thomas' benefit and Jesus blesses those who believe without seeing. We are told this is only a selection of His appearances. (20:19–30)

An appearance by the Sea of Tiberias. Peter and six others are hailed from the shore by Jesus who tells them to cast the net on the right side. The "other" recognises Jesus first. Peter then wades ashore, the others draw net and boat to shore. A meal is prepared and they have a meal from Jesus' hands. This, we are told, is the third appearance. (21:1–14)

An appearance by the sea for Peter's special benefit ("Lovest thou Me?"), ending with instructions to Peter and a prophecy about his future. He is advised not to be curious about the "other" disciple's future. (21:15–23)

Acts:

Over a period of forty days Jesus gives proofs that He is alive. He tells His disciples to wait in Jerusalem for baptism by the Holy Spirit. They ask if He will now restore the kingdom to Israel, and are told this is the Father's secret. They will be His witnesses to the ends of the earth. Jesus blesses them and disappears heavenwards. Two angels tell the disciples He will return in the same way. The disciples (men and women) devote themselves to prayer. Peter persuades them to appoint someone in Judas' place. On the Day of Pentecost the Spirit descends and Peter preaches to the multitude that Jesus is Messiah. (1:1–2:36)

1 Corinthians:

Christ rose again on the third day, according to the Scriptures. He was seen by Peter, then by the twelve. After that He was seen by more than 500 brethren at one time. After that He was seen by James and then by all the apostles. Last of all by me (Paul). (15:4–8)

It is evident there is no unanimity and the disparities in some cases are very glaring. Our sole concern at the moment is with time element. How long was it after the crucifixion before there was certainty that Jesus is risen? We cannot safely come further from the crucifixion than "the third day". Up to then there is no belief in the Risen Christ. That fixes the boundary for the crucial interval on the side nearest the crucifixion. Is there any indication that it may be impossible to be as definite on the other side? And, if this is so, will this indicate that the conviction that Jesus is risen was arrived at by a gradual process? It is with these questions in mind at present that we consider the material at our disposal.

The indications of time in the New Testament records do not permit us to conclude immediately that one interval and one only can be fixed. There are four periods to consider in view of the emphasis placed on them in the different sources. No doubt their importance in the minds of those who handed down the traditions is variously interpreted and their records are not designed to answer our special question. At this stage we simply note them as significant periods in the transition we are investigating.

Firstly, there is the period spoken of as "the third day". The calculation includes the day on which Jesus was crucified. We should say within two days of the crucifixion. It is further defined as the first day of the week.

Secondly, there is the interval which includes the disciples' journey from Jerusalem to Galilee. We have no way of being certain about the extent of this period. The disciples could have left Jerusalem immediately after Jesus was arrested, after the crucifixion, or after the third day.

Thirdly, there is a "forty-day" interval which is considered by one source to be of very exceptional importance.

Fourthly, there is a period which extends as far into the early days of the Church as the conversion of Saul. This may be as much as two years but cannot be fixed.

It will be noted that so far we have not tried to evaluate sources. We have been content simply to take all the available material and ask what answer it gives to a specific question, namely, whether there are any indications of time contained in them.

The answer, we have discovered, is four. These are (1) "the third day", (2) a time allowing for a journey from Jerusalem to Galilee, (3) the end of a forty days' interval and (4) an indefinite period whose terminus is the conversion of Saul of Tarsus.

The importance attached to these times by any of the sources is left till later, but we note these possibilities; that these times may be different answers to one question, that they may be four answers to four different questions, that they may be radically inconsistent, that they may be inconsistent due to misinterpretation of information on the part of one or other of the traditions.

One further point is to be made. It is that these times certainly take us beyond the birth moment of Christianity in the case of (4). They may do so at (3) or even at (2). They certainly do not at (1), in the sense that prior to "the third day" there was certainly no Christianity in existence.

The general and initial impression given is that the birth moment of Christianity is indefinite in terms of time but the same persons appear in the various accounts. This may point to an element of gradualness in what we are investigating and directs our attention to the possibility of persons being more significant than times and places.

CHAPTER THIRTEEN

ANALYSIS OF THE MATERIAL

IT is necessary that we should now take a closer look at the material on which any reconstruction of the critical period must be based. At this point we must begin to take note of the date and try to evaluate the quality of the material, in spite of the difficulties accompanying such a proceeding.

At the outset it must be stated that none of the documents can be exactly dated, but there is sufficient agreement among scholars to allow us to arrange them in their probable order. This order has reference to what we shall call date of publication, except in the case of the Pauline extract. We acknowledge also that the Gospels and Acts are composite works incorporating older sources, in some cases written, in others belonging to oral tradition. So it can happen that a late document may contain an early and valid tradition, perhaps in a modified form.

Our method must therefore be designed to guard against leaving us at the mercy of a matter of precise dating. So far, we have been able to avoid this possibility, but must now take the risk of being within reach of it without falling into its power.

The material is in four sections—the Pauline, the Synoptic, Acts and the Johannine. It would be generally agreed that this is the order in time. It is sufficient to place 1 Corinthians within the first two or three years of the fifth decade, Mark, Matthew and Luke within the period 70 to 85, Acts between 80 and 100 and the

Johannine Gospel in the first decade of the 2nd century. These approximate dates may not be universally agreed but the matter is not of great consequence for our purpose so long as the order is sound and the composite nature of the documents agreed.

1 Corinthians:

This is certainly the earliest material we have. It is still nearly quarter of a century after the crucial period and we have to admit possibilities of misunderstanding on the part of the author and take into account the setting of the extract. Nevertheless, the fact that it is the earliest and that it is on the precise subject advises us to treat it with great respect.

As far as the date of the events recorded is concerned, it is imprecise. The appearance to Peter and the others may have been on "the third day" or many days after. If, in one case, twelve were involved, does this imply an appearance after Judas' successor was appointed, or is it a slip, or were the twelve not yet known as apostles?

We note the only mention of James in relation to the first days. Also the identification of Paul's own experience with that of the others. The appearance to five hundred must be subsequent to the ascension if we accept Acts 1:15, where it is said, "the number of names together were about an hundred and twenty".

It is quite clear that Paul has no first-hand knowledge of this matter and is re-telling what has been reported to him. He expects his readers to believe, in reference to the first days, on the evidence on which he himself has believed. We can take it that if he had had more or more convincing evidence he would have cited it.

Mark:

It is profitless to speculate on what a lost ending of Mark would be likely to contain. We note the introduction of (three) women into the narrative and the interest in the tomb and the stone. The "and Peter" may be significant and also the intimation that the scene is to be transferred to Galilee. There is no appearance of Jesus in this account.

Matthew:

Here (two) women go to the tomb and the narrative agrees with Mark but adds that the women did see Jesus on their return journey. The repetition of the instructions at so short an interval and in such circumstances might be an indication of later addition. The Galilee scene is realised as promised. The appearance did not convince some. It may be felt that with Matthew's account we have moved further away from the bare simplicity of 1 Corinthians 15.

Luke:

Contrast the length and detail here with the Pauline account. We take note of the education of the disciples regarding the meaning of Christ's death and resurrection —on three separate occasions. Women are there but there is no appearance to them, and their story of the empty tomb is not generally believed.

The story of the Emmaus journey is unique. We note the inability to recognise Jesus and the report of the disciples that Peter (alone) has seen the Lord, in the first instance. In the final section are three additions—proof that the appearance is Jesus by sensible demonstration, the disciples forbidden to leave Jerusalem (no Galilee tradition) and the promise of power.

In Luke's narrative we feel perhaps for the first time that we are in the presence of a professional writer who has not simply told but self-consciously re-told the classic story.

John:

Much new material appears here also. Only one woman goes to the tomb. She does not at first recognise Jesus. Jesus speaks of His ascension. There are further sensible demonstrations. The Holy Spirit is conferred there and then along with power to forgive or retain sins. Two appearances are located in the north. There is a persistent attempt to thrust the "other" disciple into a place of prominence. This involves competition with Peter. It is evident that Peter's position in the crucial period is firmly established.

John's account appears to be bristling with theological and ecclesiological preoccupations. The impression is that the material is being moulded to serve other than historical or testimonial interests.

Acts:

The account here is, of course, closely related to that in Luke and in these post-crucifixion passages a similarity of style and interests is patent. Here we come upon the only mention of the forty-day period. The liaison between the end of Luke and the beginning of Acts is difficult, probably due to the introduction of the forty-day period and the necessity to record a bodily ascension. Teaching is given here also but concerning the kingdom. Peter is quite evidently the most prominent personality. The account reveals other characteristics valuable to a study of Luke–Acts but not pertinent to our immediate inquiry.

This short summary of the material shows that it grows with time, that in some respects it is far from self-consistent, that it varies according to its provenance. Bearing in mind that the earliest is a generation later than the event, though, like the others, having its roots in earlier times, it would be most rash to prefer any account out and out as against the other. A fair treatment of the material requires a much more difficult approach.

What is suggested now, therefore, is that we should make a list of the features which this survey has thrust upon our attention with a view to finding out whether a closer investigation of any or all of them can bring us any nearer a more definite picture of the first creative days. These are:

1. "The Third Day".
2. The Tomb and the Women.
3. Jerusalem and/or Galilee.
4. The Element of Unbelief.
5. Education on the Cross and Resurrection.
6. The Prominence of Peter.

We may treat (1) and (2) very briefly in this chapter, but the others will require much more detailed attention. They will involve us in an attempt to get inside the minds of the disciples during the significant period. This in turn will require some treatment of the expectations of the disciples prior to the crucifixion. Meantime we turn to "The Third Day" and "The Tomb and the Women".

The Third Day

There is every reason to believe that "the third day" was conventional from an early date. It is so in the

Epistles of Paul, and this is confirmed by the formula, "according to the scriptures". It is not difficult to see how this would happen.

No one, apparently, could testify to seeing Jesus actually rising from the dead. This would have been the ultimate in testimony and, had it been available, it would certainly have been quoted from the very beginning. The next immediate possibility was to be aware that Jesus had just risen. The closer such witness approached the actual dividing line between death and life, the more striking it would appear and therefore the more effective as testimony.

It is evident, therefore, that the tradition regarding the resurrection could be pressed no further than the earliest moment after the actual event. And, in the nature of the case, it was inevitable that this should in fact happen. The tradition could not come to a state of rest until that point had been reached. It is the only position for a *terminus a quo* for a completed corpus of resurrection narrative.

"The third day" is not stated by Paul to be the date of the first appearance. We have seen that this question of time and place is not one which requires precision as far as he is concerned. It is sufficient for him that others are reported to have seen the Lord—as he himself has. That their experience preceded his own is neither here nor there and in no way distinguishes them from him. He has seen Christ as well as they.

In Mark "the third day" is still not the date of the first appearance: it is the date of preparation for appearance. But this is to take place only after the disciples have made the seventy-mile journey from Jerusalem to Galilee. It might be inferred that the appearances of Jesus belong not to the story of Jesus but to the story of the Church.

The other traditions are in complete agreement in setting down a confident and detailed account of events on "the third day", even to the point of stating in some cases the particular hour of the day. The accounts are not consistent but they are precise beyond anything in Paul and Mark. And they record appearances up to the earliest moment possible. This reveals progression in the tradition in accordance with the dogmatic expectation described above. It is evident therefore that the resurrection tradition could have developed up to a precise position in the matter of time and that it did this very thing. In retrospect this position was bound to become the initial moment of the complete tradition regarding the whole event, the birth-hour of belief in the Risen Lord.

Once the necessity for a starting point is evident, it is readily fixed by predetermining and dogmatic necessities. It was not possible to go back beyond the supposed dividing line between life and death. An hour after the expiry, for instance, would certainly render the probability of a genuine death and resurrection suspect. If there is evidence of a belief that a certain period elapsed before the soul finally departed from the lifeless body, then that would determine the utmost reach of any resurrection narrative—the third day. Such evidence may be present in John 11:39.

Other influences would confirm this; for instance, scriptural analogy. A passage such as Hosea 6:2 must have been full of significance to a generation which gathered testimonies as proofs of Jesus' Messiahship from the Old Testament Scriptures in the fashion illustrated in Matthew's Gospel, for instance. In the reference to Jonah's being three days in the belly of the whale (Matthew 12:40) we have a very precise and ingenious instance. This passage (Matthew 12:38–42) is usually assigned to Q and paralleled in Luke 11:29–32. But Luke includes no reference to "three days". Jonah's mission is to warn of coming judgment, not to typify the resurrection. At some stage, presumably later than Q, this resurrection reference entered the tradition. But "the third day" was already conventional.

The Tomb and the Women

We have already seen that the tomb plays no part in the early belief in the resurrection. The further we go from the date of the event, the more focal does the tomb become. This is to be expected. Tradition sharpens the total picture till both time and place have become precisely fixed and what is initially insignificant is burdened with a weight it was never expected to bear. The vague "somewhere" and "somewhen" is now "there" and "then".

This, it should be remarked, is not a surmise but a deduction from the material. The place is predetermined in precisely the same fashion as the time and, of course, must be co-ordinated with it. Documents are vague or silent as to both or clear and definite as to both. Paul has no mention of the tomb and "the third day" as we have seen is conventional; Peter's reported speech mentions neither. On the other hand the Gospels give increasingly factual and pointed prominence to both.

We know nothing of how those who incurred the full penalty of the criminal law were disposed of after their execution. Perhaps this has little bearing on what befell the body of one in particular. But if the earliest records tell us nothing on the subject, we must be cautious in accepting complete accounts coming from a much later period, especially if there existed a dogmatic gap requiring to be filled.

It follows that to try to answer such questions as "Who moved the stone?", is a speculation on a proposition which is itself speculative in the first place, and therefore a proceeding which can hardly be expected to establish any useful conclusion.

The presence of women in the later stories is not quite in the same category. That they should be represented as going to the tomb to embalm or to weep over the body of Jesus without making provision for admission to the tomb is of a piece with the tomb tradition in the sense that it shows a growing point of the same organon.

However, the difficulty is in the fact that they are present at all. It seems impossible that they should be introduced into the story at a later stage in the tradition, and we must conclude that they were present in the initial moments of the belief.

The part they played shows development even within the Synoptic Gospels. In Mark there is no appearance to women. An angel informs them at the tomb of the great event. Matthew adds that on the way back Jesus Himself met and spoke with them. Luke enhances the story in the same direction. The Fourth Gospel adds its own even more precise details.

The association of women with the story, therefore, is that they went to find the body of Jesus and did not succeed. When and where, it may not be possible to determine in view of the necessities which pressed ever more heavily upon the two factors of time and place in the developing tradition. We are therefore, it would seem, bound to admit the presence of women at the beginning, but that they went to a tomb and that on the third day would require earlier and better testimony.

CHAPTER FOURTEEN

LOCATION OF THE APPEARANCES

WHEN we come to consider where the reported appearance of Christ after His resurrection took place, we reach a point at which the traditional theologian most violently rebels against the historical approach to this subject. It is safe to say that, if all the records were in perfect agreement as to the location of these appearances, the witness of the historian would be welcomed. The fact is that no one can make all our authorities tell the same or even a consistent story. The gap between them is not simply a question of disparities but of contradictions.

Let us consider what this problem permits and does not permit us to do. If it is to be maintained that after His death Jesus made Himself known by appearing in some form to His disciples, and that this was not a matter of psychological awareness on the part of the disciples but of substantive proof conveyed by Jesus, then this is history in the same sense as the crucifixion is history and subject therefore to the same kind of historical investigation.

It follows from this that both theologians and historians are bound by certain conditions. If the theologian is anxious to maintain the historicity of the resurrection, he must not try to rail off the post-crucifixion period from historical investigation. He must not allow, for instance, freedom to decide whether the cleansing of the temple took place at the beginning or the end of Jesus' ministry as a historical issue, but at the same time refuse to allow any decision on historical grounds as to where and when Jesus appeared after His crucifixion.

Conversely, if the theologian is anxious to withdraw the resurrection from the province of the historian (for dogmatic reasons or in view of the contradictions, for example), he must rest his case for belief in the Risen Jesus on a base not subject to historical scrutiny. If he says, "I believe because Peter or some other has reported," he must be content to allow the query whether it is true that Peter or some other has in fact done so. This is a historical inquiry. If he says, "I believe because I experience," this is a matter of religious psychology. But he cannot use his faith in the resurrection as both a religious experience and an acceptance of a historical fact to forbid the investigation of the data from a historical point of view.

The historian is similarly situated. As historian he is not in a position to start the history of the Church from an assumption of miracle, unless he can prove that it has no explanation in terms of other historical events. It will not do to tell the story of Jesus up to the crucifixion, interpolate a paragraph intimating a supra-historical event which cannot be described, and begin the Church's history from, for example, the Day of Pentecost, if, on the plane of history, he believes there is continuity between the life of Jesus and the beginnings of Church history. History has no gaps. It cannot be written on the assumption of discontinuity.

It is regrettable that many theologians and Church historians have never frankly recognised these conditions imposed by their disciplines. In view of the nature of the data of this period, they have both been anxious to secure the best of both worlds. The theologian wants a historical basis for his doctrine without the necessity to submit to the conditions of historical investigation. The Church historian has often been content to begin Church history as if a dogmatic basis were the equivalent in Church history of a historical basis in any other historical investigation. But, if we go in terror lest history disprove faith, then we are of all men most miserable.

We have seen that our earliest sources (the speeches of Peter in Acts and St. Paul's record in 1 Cor. 15) tell us nothing regarding time and place in relation to the post-crucifixion appearances. As to our other authorities, Mark records no appearance but forecasts a meeting of Jesus and His disciples in Galilee; Matthew inserts an appearance to women in Jerusalem and relates an appearance in Galilee; Luke–Acts recounts appearances in the Jerusalem area and records an expressed command to the disciples not to leave Jerusalem; John records appearances both in Jerusalem and in Galilee.

The most obtrusive fact here is the isolation in which Luke–Acts stands as strictly confining all activities to the Jerusalem area. This is done not by default (as might be argued in the case of Mark's omission of all reference to Jerusalem appearances) but deliberately, and in such a way as to put the matter beyond all doubt.

The questions raised by this fact are much wider than our own concern. They must be taken into account in any estimate of the authorship and provenance of Luke–Acts. In their simplest form they are: Why does Luke–Acts confine appearances to Jerusalem? Was this a deliberate attempt to displace any tradition relating them to the north? How does it reflect on the historical reliability of Luke–Acts? Does it indicate a fluid state of post-crucifixion tradition of such a nature as to discredit all attempts to locate appearances?

We are brought to such a pass in this investigation that

it is difficult to decide how to proceed. Evidently no one
can rest content with a vague notion that something
happened but we know not what. Again, it is not possible
to create a picture of this period in which every recorded
incident will somehow find a place. Historically this is a
position in which the records themselves compel us to
discriminate against some or perhaps all of them.

Clearly it will not do simply to set aside Luke–Acts
and try to harmonise the others into a consistent record.
That, for one thing, is to treat part of a tradition as if it
were the whole just for the sake of consistency. It is too
easy—but, more important, it would not be honest—to
work out the sum without taking the surd into account.
This is evidently a proposition in which arbitrary selection
of some data, even if it were legitimate, would not produce a reasonable conclusion. The indications are that a
fundamental hypothesis of the documents themselves is
at fault.

Luke–Acts succeeds in providing a consecutive story
by confining the disciples in Jerusalem from the time of
the crucifixion to the Day of Pentecost. But in order to do
so he has to depart from the other tradition or traditions
in a radical fashion. Even so, the junction between Luke
and Acts is not perfect. There is no suggestion in the last
verses of Luke that the ascension took place only after
a period of forty days during which appearances of an
unmistakable nature took place.

If we isolate what is peculiar to Luke–Acts, we have
to include the following: the Emmaus incident, repeated
instruction on the necessity for the death and resurrection and its Old Testament authority, the command to
wait in Jerusalem for power, repeated proofs over a
period of forty days, the actual ascension, the Day of
Pentecost. This is surely a very formidable tradition and

it makes all the more drastic the necessity to consider discarding it.

We should note here that, if we subtract the last chapter of the Fourth Gospel as redactional, we are left with the fact that this Gospel originally had no account of appearances in the north. Luke–Acts therefore is not in the position of being an individualist reconstruction of events. It is representative of a stream of tradition—which admitted no reference to Galilean appearances. The fact that the final chapter was added in the later edition of the Fourth Gospel, means that accommodation had to be made between two traditions at least. This again means that the state of post-crucifixion tradition in at least one Christian centre was still fluid into the beginning of the second century.

If, however, we refuse to discard the "Jerusalem only" tradition, our other sources, which all contain references to appearances in Galilee, must be allowed to fall. This alternative is equally drastic, especially when we recall Luke's primary dependence on Mark for the basic outline of the life and last days of Jesus. We are thus in a cleft stick.

What we are investigating at present is the location of the assurance which created the Church in the first place. We are at a stand. Let us, then, remind ourselves that this is only part of our total subject which must embrace these three questions: Where did this occur? What was its nature? Who were its instruments? Our sources do not give a direct and unambiguous answer to the first question. If we press the question we find ourselves being forced to choose between two incompatible traditions. But we cannot feel justified in making such a choice.

It would seem, therefore, that we must either approach the question *de novo* on the basis of probability, or come to the conclusion that there is something which is inherently self-contradictory in the accounts themselves, or both. We cannot be satisfied to leave a historical investigation in a condition of such patent incongruity, especially when the incongruity arises out of our original data. Contradictions may equally be reactions to the same basic event. Only when we have discovered what the basic event is, are we aware of their relation and explanation.

The post-crucifixion accounts cannot be understood except in the light of answers to the three questions above (What happened? Where? And to whom?), for they are effects deriving from the event itself. Conversely, from our side, the event itself is only arrived at through the account. This means that whatever solution we arrive at of the total problem must reveal both event and consequents as coherent circumstances in which contradictions find a necessary explanation.

We proceed first of all on the more limited investigation, namely that regarding the location of appearances, on the basis of probability. Is it possible to say where the initial events constituting the Church as a new movement in history took place?

The choice between Galilee and Jerusalem is formidable. Are we bound to make it, or is there some answer to the question, What, in fact, happened?, which will admit of an answer requiring both locations?

There are events of this nature. The beginning of a new king's reign, for example, might conceivably lead to such a double emphasis. The question, When was the king crowned? can have only one precise answer, but, When did he become king? might not. It might be answered by giving the moment when the old king died or by giving the date of the coronation. The question has, so to speak, both a private and a public answer. In some such way the answer to the question, When was Christianity born? might have a private and a public answer in which both Galilee and Jerusalem are involved as locations.

It is therefore not impossible that our variant traditions are due to a difference in emphasis which permits two answers to a question because the question is differently understood by the two traditions. The one answers Galilee and the other Jerusalem. It may be that they are dealing with a consecutive event. *In toto* it requires both locations, but what happened in each location is distinct from what happened in the other. If this composite and consecutive nature of the event is not realised, it is easy to conceive how the two component traditions will become rival. Both will claim priority under the impression that they are speaking of the same event which they consider unitary.

Let us suppose that this total event, which is distinguished by two consecutive points of emphasis, is regarded as the fact that Jesus is risen or the fact that the Church is born. All accounts of resurrection appearances in our material would then be regarded as answers to the question: When and where did it happen? The answers are two: Galilee, Jerusalem. We need not concern ourselves with the fact that one tradition is obviously aggressive in its anxiety to exclude the other. This is natural and readily explicable in the circumstances we postulate.

Now if one tradition arose through concentration on the primary fact that the first awareness of the total event must have been private, and the other through concentration on the fact that the reference of the total event is public, indeed universal, then we are able to see how both arose and how both grew in importance side by side. Both could be true but they are not referring to precisely the same circumstance, although to the same event.

Luke–Acts' emphasis on Jerusalem is completely understandable on this hypothesis. The author maintains that the Church was born, as an agent of the Gospel in the world, at Jerusalem on the Day of Pentecost. Significantly, it is he who refuses to countenance any reference to appearances in Galilee. His account of the appearances is entirely consistent with his thesis that Jerusalem is both the birthplace and the headquarters of the Church. If the Luke–Acts documents had not maintained the Jerusalem reference in regard to the appearances, our two-part event hypothesis would not have stood.

But the public manifestation of the event must be subsequent to the private aspect—indeed, consequent on it. The beginning of the Church as the agent of the Gospel in the world is possible only because the necessary dynamic for its creation is already a reality in someone's consciousness. And it is this facet of the event which is creative to the Galilee tradition. Priority in time belongs to Galilee. Priority in importance as far as Luke–Acts is concerned belongs to Jerusalem. These two priorities are not mutually exclusive. The total event embraces them both.

As regards the priority in time of the Galilee portion of the total event, there is every necessary support for it. It is practically impossible to reverse the order, unless we are prepared to renounce the whole framework of Luke–Acts. The Jerusalem tradition can be understood if it follows the Galilee tradition, but not vice versa.

Without going into a detailed examination of the pre-crucifixion story, it will be admitted that the disciples looked upon Jesus' journey to Jerusalem with foreboding, that Jesus never visualised the death of any of them along with Himself as a consequence, that the Last Supper was (whatever else) a farewell meal, that there was no expectation they should remain in Jerusalem after the arrest of Jesus (since they did not then believe in His resurrection) and that the danger of their being taken into custody, contrary to the expressed wish of their Master, was considered to be very real. All these facts, each of which might well be amplified, make it highly probable that the disciples did not remain in Jerusalem from the arrest to the Day of Pentecost. They fled. Whither? There can be only one answer. It explains why in the first instance it was not possible to represent men as being among those who sought for the body of Jesus on the third day.

What happened in Galilee we are not yet in a position to discuss. But that the initial thing, without which there would be no Christian Church, took place in the north, there seems no reason to doubt. And that this was followed by a starkly public event in Jerusalem is the logical conclusion from our evidence.

Acts presents a picture of the disciples existing furtively in Jerusalem till the Day of Pentecost, whereupon with great boldness they publicly declare their faith that Jesus is risen. The contrast is deliberate. But, if our reconstruction is correct so far, the most amazing thing that took place was not a public demonstration in a state of exultation, but the seventy-mile return journey of the disciples from Galilee to Jerusalem where, on their last unforgettable visit, Jesus had been crucified.

So often in tradition the nuance is right but the accent is in the wrong place. This can explain the double tradition regarding the appearances and also the contrast between a fearful little group in Jerusalem and a band of new-inspired men walking back to the city which had crucified their Lord.

CHAPTER FIFTEEN

THE ELEMENT OF UNBELIEF

BECAUSE we are now about to enter a different phase of our investigation it will be convenient to review the phase through which we have passed. We began by delimiting the area with which we are concerned. It is the shortest interval between the time when it is possible to say, No Christianity exists yet and the time when it can be said, Christianity is now in existence. What happened within that interval is our subject, in other words the birth of the Christian faith.

We found that the conventional limits of this interval are from "the third day" to the "Day of Pentecost". Within that period, our records inform us, relations between Jesus (who had been crucified) and His disciples were renewed. An analysis of the records revealed that there are not only disparities but contradictions. These presuppose a growth in tradition regarding what took place. This required that "the third day" must be the conventional beginning. The traditions themselves predispose us to consider the total event as one which is capable of a double, consecutive emphasis. This is the only premise which can account for the contradictions, in particular with regard to the location of appearances.

We have shown reason to believe that after the crucifixion the disciples returned to Galilee, and that it is there and then that we must find the initial indication of the event we call the birth of the Christian faith.

In the course of our analysis of the material at our disposal we found that we are trying to come to grips with one event which requires for its understanding the answers to three questions. These are:

1. Where and when did it occur?
2. What was its nature?
3. Who were its instruments?

So far we have dealt with the first of these only. We now proceed to consider the whole subject, not in terms of time and place, but primarily in terms of the nature of the occurrence to which tradition bears witness.

It will be recalled that all the matters so far dealt with arise directly out of a close examination of the records. Among the points we noted as prominent features of the whole corpus of tradition, were "the third day", the women and the tomb, Jerusalem and/or Galilee. These we have now reviewed and the next is the title of this chapter—the element of unbelief.

It will readily be seen that with this subject we are indeed entering on a new phase. It is new in two respects. Up to now we have been concentrating on time and place; now our attention is on event. Up to now our primary interest has been in the external scene; now we turn to the experience.

It is true that these are not separable: experience and event take place in time and space whatever else may be said about them. Our plea has been for the recognition of this fact as opposed to the tendency to introduce discontinuity into the experience and so make time and place irrelevant. We consider them separately because this is how they arise in the course of investigation, not because we imagine they are independent of each other. The stage is set before the play begins; no play can be played nowhere. Appearances and experiences must take place in the life of someone at some place, and to this general truth the records bear witness.

But having said this, we are not thereby obliged to conclude that the records of the event with which we have to do are *ipso facto* complete and beyond the reach of examination. Especially is this so since, as is the case, no *prima facie* consistency arises out of them. This is precisely the matter on which we are now engaged.

Our traditions present us with this unexpected and unexplained fact. The central constituent of the total event was not self-evidencing to all who were confronted with it. Some did not believe, did not know, did not recognise, required further proof. Why was this so? What light does it throw upon the nature of the occurrence? What new kind of demonstration was possible or what could a time-interval effect in order that unbelief should become belief or failure to recognise become recognition?

These are very perplexing questions if we elect to take the accounts simply at their face value. We are in the presence of a direct encounter between persons well known to each other. It would seem impossible in the nature of the case that time or repetition could do what the initial person-to-person relationship had failed to do. Yet there is no question of disguise or deliberate attempt to confuse. On the contrary, the declared purpose of the appearances is to assure and convince, and the *raison d'etre* of the record of the whole encounter is frustrated if this is not so.

This difficulty is sometimes explained away by postulating a state of mind (in those who were not convinced) which made the exercise of ordinary faculties of recognition unreliable. But such a presupposition raises more problems than it solves. Why, for instance, the discrimination as between persons passing through a common experience and confronted with the same phenomenon? Is it the distrait or the other who recognises, believes, requires no further proof? It would be difficult on this ground to withstand the argument that hallucination explains all.

Once again there is the temptation to give up the quest for a continuous account of the event to which our records unanimously if confusedly point back. It met us when we considered the discrepancies in the matter of time, and again in the matter of place. Now, when we ask What did occur? we are confronted with the same inducement to retire and hand the whole matter over to the theologians, who will claim the event as historical but not subject to historical investigation.

If we refuse to deliver this foundational episode over to contingency, we must begin by realising clearly the situation in which we find ourselves. It is impossible to accept the records as they stand as a self-consistent account of the event. This has been freely recognised by scholars for many years. The element of unbelief is inexplicable if it refers to the recognition of a person who is presumed to be intent on establishing his identity in the presence of intimate friends.

This presumption, which is inalienable from the records, may appear to some to be questionable. But there is no way of establishing personal identity in a matter like this except through likeness at the very least. If certainty is required, and the sources insist on certainty (i.e. it was not someone like Jesus but Jesus Himself), then even likeness is not sufficient. Nothing less than identity in the sense of one-and-the-sameness will do. Jesus could not convince His disciples that He was Jesus by appearing to be quite unlike Jesus. Yet the records require that to some He should be certainly identical with

Jesus, but to others at the same time He should not even resemble Himself.

Such contradictions cannot be resolved on the basic assumption—that He appeared in corporeal form to His disciples. Must we then abandon the assumption? This, it should be noted, would not require us to adopt a theory of hallucination. It need not commit us, and indeed must not, to any conclusion which is not sufficient to account not only for the existence of the traditions but for the growth of those traditions in particular.

Two facts must be reckoned with, facts which our earlier assumption of bodily appearances cannot cope with: (1) the possibility of opposite conclusions existing side by side in relation to the event, i.e. this is Jesus and this is not Jesus, and (2) the possibility that time can have any effect on the conclusions, i.e. that some did not believe initially but later were quite convinced, when in fact nothing different had happened external to themselves to account for the change.

These two facts are related primarily to the apprehension of the disciples. In no case in the tradition (except, perhaps, in the Fourth Gospel and in apparent recognition of this precise difficulty) is the bodily appearance represented as subject to unpredictable alteration in form. The emphasis of the tradition in this respect is upon the ability or otherwise of the disciples to recognise that the appearance is the appearance of Jesus. There seems to be nothing which the appearance could do to convince the unconvinced except simply to be itself, i.e. the appearance of Jesus. Belief and unbelief is not equated in the records with more likeness or less likeness to Jesus in appearance. It is the personal reaction of the disciple to the fact in whose presence he stands.

This means that the belief or unbelief is not represented

as a matter of overriding compulsion from without, but that it is a conclusion arrived at by normal human process as far as it applies to conviction and belief. It is belief not by fiat but by conclusion, by reaching that point along the normal psychological pathway that habitually leads to belief. The content of this belief is not yet our concern. We are merely establishing that the upshot of the event which is enshrined in the traditions was, in fact, a conviction arrived at in the same way as any human conviction is arrived at.

It is necessary to recapitulate the argument to this point. Among those present at the critical time and place were some who did not believe. This is so embarrassing to the later tradition that it must be regarded as of great authenticity. Since the purpose of the appearance as recorded is to convince and any attempt to confuse is excluded, we must conclude that the passage from unbelief to belief, from failure to recognise to recognition, was due to modification in the mind of those concerned and not to variation in the phenomenon itself. It is represented in this way in the record.

But if what we have called the phenomenon was a bodily appearance of Jesus, it is impossible, as has been shown, to account for the element of unbelief. We are therefore under the necessity to modify the assumption. But such modification must account for the traditions and for those features of the traditions which it is impossible to accommodate.

The suggestion is made, therefore, that all these factors are immediately seen to be congruous if the effective phenomenon at the very centre is not a bodily appearance which results in questions as to whether "it" is there or not or whether "it" is identifiable or not, but a new conception of who and what Jesus is.

We arrive at the conclusion, therefore, that what occurred at the critical time and place was not simply an
appearance which is capable of being testified to by those
who witness it, and denied by those who do not, but a
revelation of truth which is capable of being simultaneously apprehended by some and not by others initially, but later is truly apprehended by all. If it is felt
that something other than this must be postulated in
addition, it should be noted that this "other" is not
necessary to account for the records and indeed, of itself,
is not capable of doing so. It should further be noted
that the appearance interpreted as corporeal is not necessary to account for the belief, but, contrariwise, the belief
may very well account for the records of bodily appearance.

This latter statement may appear to be the complete
contrary of the general appraisal of the matter. But if the
statement is considered, it is simply an assessment that
any man who rises from the dead is not the Christ of the
Christian faith. The core of the whole event is the question, Who and what is Jesus? The answer to such a
question cannot be found in a post-crucifixion appearance
in isolation. It is the conclusion of a process of intense
preoccupation with the known facts of the life of Jesus.
It is impossible to cut the birth of the faith off from the
active ministry of Jesus and the association of disciples
with Him in the period before His death. The Church
was conceived during His ministry though it was not
born till after His death.

What the content of the revelation or conviction was,
we must leave to the next chapter. But it is conceivable
that it was such that it could not be expressed except in
terms of a nature which accounts for the traditions. It is
extremely difficult for us to appreciate the thought-forms

of Palestine in the 1st century. This is admitted in the interpretation of the sayings of Jesus. It would be agreed that resurrection itself in the Hebrew connotation is a category alien to Graeco-Roman thought. Did it express in the pre-Christian tradition something which had no counterpart in the thought of any other people?

We read in the Old Testament of a prophet besieged by foreign troops. The heart of his servant sank. The prophet prayed: "Lord, I pray Thee, open his eyes that he may see." The narrative continues: "And the Lord opened the eyes of the young man; and he saw: and, behold, the mountain was full of horses and chariots of fire round about Elisha" (2 Kings 6:17). It may be asked whether we know what this means and if so whether we should express it in the same way.

The possibility is that no other way was open to express what happened at the birth of Christianity except the way that was taken. And this in itself would be a measure of the unprecedented nature of the occurrence. The expression of some experience hitherto beyond knowledge and belief creates its own problem. How can one express what has never been expressed before? The choice is silence or the extravagant use of what has been already known or believed. The choice of silence was not open to the disciples.

CHAPTER SIXTEEN

EVENT OR CONVICTION?

WE have been forced to the conclusion that bodily appearances cannot account for the form and content of the traditions in the post-crucifixion story. It has been argued that the phenomenon at the centre of the traditions is not an objective event but a conviction arrived at by normal process and that this explains the patent discrepancies of the traditions.

The resurrection regarded as an objective event is thought to be so central to the Christian theology that this interpretation must be prepared to meet massive traditional and psychological opposition. We therefore pause here to consider whether it is possible to maintain our position.

To the theologian the resurrection is autogenous and *a priori*. It is a new, miraculous, historically uncaused phenomenon which initiates consequences but can have no mundane antecedents. Christian doctrine has accordingly concentrated almost exclusively on what can be deduced therefrom and scarcely at all on the context in which it is found. The comparative neglect of the bearing of inter-Testamental Jewish theology on this matter by all but a few scholars proves this.

Can one maintain the historicity of an event which is conceived as having none of its causes in time and most of its consequences in supra-mundane terms? Could such an event be integrated into meaningful relation with the rest of life? Now we know of no effect in history which has God for its sole cause. And to postulate such an event would be to substitute supposition for necessary connexion in a case in which necessary connexion alone will be sufficient.

Before a dogmatic pronouncement which precludes investigation of possible causes is accepted, the history and context of an idea or event should be examined. If this door is closed to the historian, it is closed also to the theologian. The latter will no longer be able to claim an effective relationship between doctrine and meaningful existence. The theologian will have become a theosophist.

Consequently, if belief in the resurrection is claimed to be more than a fascinating speculation, the historical approach is imperative. And once it is permitted it may or may not confirm the doctrine to which the theologian is committed. Certainly by its nature it cannot be bound to do so.

In the remainder of this chapter, therefore, I propose to do two things. The first is to review briefly the history of the idea of resurrection in the pre-Christian period, the second is to remark on the alleged psychological necessity for some kind of objectivity in the experience of the disciples in the post-crucifixion period, even when the belief in physical resurrection has been surrendered. This is often urged as an argument for a position imagined to lie between the Scylla of hallucination and the Charybdis of resurrection of the flesh.

The idea of resurrection is strictly dependent on the idea of God; eschatology is an outgrowth from theology. To put it more concretely by example, you cannot believe in eternal punishment unless your God allows you to do so.

But theology does not immediately and automatically affect eschatology. There is a time-lag. Ultimately a genuine belief in God permeates all—worship, ethics, eschatology. But it often happens that the full impact of a theology is only potential. Thus a professed belief in God may live side by side with an incompatible ethic or eschatology which belongs with and arises from a more primitive conception of God.

The doctrine of God takes time to modify the various departments of our thought. It would seem to affect our ideas about the future life last of all.

Old Testament history had run most of its course before belief in resurrection was possible. Sheol dominated eschatology even when the 8th-century prophets had enlarged and ennobled the Hebrew conception of God. Men continued to feel bound to see God's justice and mercy worked out in their present life, for beyond was only the literally God-forsaken barrenness of the underworld.

The breakthrough came in two directions—in the direction of the thrust first of national hope and second of individual hope. The development of eschatological beliefs was a dynamic result of the frustrations of practical experience (both in national and in individual history) and the invincible hope in God which would not allow that frustration is the meaning of life.

The upshot is first, belief in a coming kingdom on the earth in which the nation will be justified before the world and enjoy abundant prosperity and, secondly, belief in a blessed immortality for the individual man whose whole trust is in God. It is the meeting of these two that generates belief in resurrection. Individual saints are to be raised to enjoy the blessings of the kingdom on earth with those alive at the time. This is a bodily resurrection on this earth to an earthly kingdom which will last for ever.

But further experience continues to modify eschatology. It comes to be thought that this world can never be suitable for an eternal kingdom of God. This thought makes possible many variations on the theme of what must come to pass. The creation of a new heaven and a new earth, the limited duration of the earthly kingdom, the extended scope of the resurrection, these and many other new conceptions found a place in the eschatological programmes of the time.

It is recognised that out of the profusion of eschatological agitation between 200 B.C. and A.D. 100 many rival schedules of the course of future events were drawn up. The questions at issue were numerous. They were widely and vigorously debated. We should be mistaken in supposing that only professional theologians and book-producers discussed the nature of the Coming Kingdom, the resurrection body and the God-appointed Man.

These are matters on which it is not possible or necessary to discover a consensus of opinion or to excogitate consistency. Hopes take small account of incompatibilities. It is only necessary to recognise that this is the fervent and turbid background against which the New Testament teaching on eschatology and resurrection must take its place.

Belief in the resurrection of Jesus in particular did not, perhaps could not, arise except where there already existed belief in resurrection in general. This is not to say that the one created the other, which is hardly possible. But one is the context of the other and to that extent a cause.

In those eschatologies which foretold an eternal kingdom in a new heaven and new earth, it is the reclothed spirit that is the bearer of personality. The present body cannot enter this kingdom any more than the present earth can be its locus. It is the kingdom of glory and all who dwell in it are likewise glorified.

When we inquire concerning the eschatology of Jesus on the evidence of the Synoptic Gospels, it is apparent that it postulated a new heaven and new earth, preceded by a time of trouble culminating in universal judgment. The Law will abide till heaven and earth pass away. The righteous shall shine as the sun (be glorious) in the kingdom of their Father. There are frequent references to a time of catastrophe. The theme of judgment in which the righteous are welcomed to everlasting glory and the wicked depart to everlasting doom is prominent.

Regarding the nature of resurrection in Gospel teaching, the evidence is that those who enter into eternal life do so in a transformed mode of existence. The present body is of so little account that it is not to be saved and its loss is not to be feared. The main aim is to live so faithfully that it is possible to enter into the life to come.

In argument with the Sadducees Jesus says the life to come is like that of the angels, a different order of being from man. This passage (Mark 12:18–27 and parallels) is followed by an interesting exposition which implies that resurrection is not always essential. Abraham and the patriarchs are now alive in God's presence, i.e. before the resurrection period. Jesus argues not that the dead are raised but that (at least some of) the dead live. This is not exceptional since there is evidence of similar belief regarding Enoch, Moses and Elijah.

The absence of consistency we have noted seems to have prevailed in the early Church. Resurrection was confidently expected as a prelude to the kingdom, but the temporary fate of the believer who died in the meantime could not be left in abeyance. The question was vigorously discussed in Corinth and it would be rash to assume that Paul's was the only or even a generally accepted answer. In Philippians 1:23 it is said that to depart this life is to be with Christ—even before the time at which the dead in Christ are to be raised. The dying thief could be with Christ on that very day without, apparently, a resurrection experience in the conventional sense.

What these considerations seem to make plain is that the teaching about resurrection in the 1st century was not a unity. It was a congeries of thought belonging to different stages of development in which the primitive reposed side by side with the most advanced. Systematic eschatology was, perhaps must be, impossible.

As regards the teaching of Jesus, there are indications that the centre of interest was not the mode of transition to eternal life but the urgency of attaining it. The word "resurrection" is not of frequent occurrence and is used probably always in answer to a question. (Curious questions are positively discouraged.) While it is precarious to draw strict conclusions from this it can hardly be argued that this precise subject of resurrection was prominent in His teaching.

The life to be lived now, in order to attain the life to come which is a transformed existence, looms large. It is far from clear that this life to come depends on the act and fact of resurrection rather than on the established relationship with God, as in the prophets and psalmists.

If we suppose Jesus to have told His disciples He would rise on the third day (and this is fraught with grave objections), it is not proved that He encouraged them to expect resuscitation such as the later Gospel tradition insists on. The Church's subsequent canonisation of the doctrine of the resurrection of the flesh (modified to body), arose from dogmatic necessity—the need to combat Gnosticism made it doubly necessary.

Now there are three general reflections that arise from a study of this subject of resurrection. The first is that it

was not and could not be deduced from experience; it was
not an intellectual conclusion on the basis of evidence,
but was born of the proleptic reach of faith. It was not so
much something drawn out of experience as something
thrown ahead so as to be joyfully encountered in experience yet to come. Briefly, the doctrine of resurrection
is in the first instance the creation of the human spirit in
its relation to God and the future.

Secondly, the thought was clothed in whatever garment
was appropriate and available at the particular time. This
depended on what would be allowed by the believer's
doctrine of God, the world and man; and this was a
matter in which variation was possible and took place.
Bodily and spiritual resurrection lived side by side in the
same period. The range is from the Sadducees who re-
nounced all apocalyptic speculation, to those who tended
to regard the mode of resurrection as entirely secondary
or even substituted immortality for resurrection.

This brings us to the third fact, which is that the essence
and content of the doctrine is a union with God that nothing can destroy. This is the primal faith which expressed
itself in relation to the future as the doctrine of resurrection. It is not itself a hope but a present reality. It gives
rise to a hope and that hope expresses what the present
reality will ultimately be seen to be when it has inevitably
won its victory over every possible impediment.

It is therefore evident that resurrection is not so much a
proof of the inviolability of God's relation with the believer, as an inference therefrom. From the manward side
it is not an event which leads to the conclusion that there
is life after death: it is itself a conclusion from the present
faith that nothing shall separate us from the love of God.

This is the context of New Testament resurrection. It
is a fulfilment of prophecy and apocalyptic, in line with

the history of the idea and having the same content and the same origin, the garment in which it is clothed, as ever, being conditioned and secondary. Great spiritual convictions which are the fruit of ventures of faith are not readily inherited. They tend to be absorbed by being reduced to their most public and least strenuous formula. The greatest are most likely to suffer from crass material-isation.

The conclusion therefore that this phenomenon at the centre of the post-crucifixion experience of the disciples is a conviction rather than an event is continuous with what we have found in our survey of the history of the resurrec-tion idea. Historical necessity wove the garment. The Christian conviction survived, but in a grosser form and at the expense of the pure leap of faith which is its source and origin. It survived more as a *modus operandi dei* than as a creative inspiration of the soul thirled to God. Hence the mechanical aridity of most subsequent eschato-logical teaching.

It is now time to turn to the question of objectivity. Many who have discarded the grosser conception of resurrection still wish to cling to what they consider to be the necessity for an objective event "of some kind".

It is not clear what is meant by objectivity in this con-text. An underlying assumption seems to be that what is not external to oneself is illusory. Nothing "real" can happen apart from external stimulus. This involves a psycho-physical theory which in another context would be regarded as an extreme form of behaviourism.

The most urgent psychological need for objectivity is felt to arise from the supposed impossibility of accounting for the transformation in the disciples apart from some supernatural event. But this change is itself subjective. Is it to be argued that every such change is the result of

external event? Would it be argued theologically that the
Holy Spirit never operates except via an objective agency
of special competence, i.e. not related to the normal context of life?

Let us consider the transformation. This tends to be
placed in a special category for two reasons—its dramatic
intensity and its spectacular character. As regards the
first, how much depends on the assumption that it took
place in the space of three days at most? Yet this cannot
have been the case. The whole narrative is foreshortened
in the Gospels and thereby sharpened to an unnatural
degree. Nothing prevents us from assuming the time
necessary for a crisis of conviction to run its course.

If the vitality of the contrast between pre-crucifixion
and post-crucifixion reactions is thus modified, it is also
due to be modified still further in terms of its own content. It is generally assumed that the cause of the disciples'
dejection was related to Jesus directly. But this is not so.
It was related to their own psychological circumstances.
Their disappointment and disillusion was with the course
of events, with the part they had played, with the part of
their rulers and with the fate of Jesus. But it cannot for a
moment be maintained that they were disappointed in
what Jesus was in Himself. Had it been otherwise no
miracle could have restored faith in Him.

Once this distinction is made clear, it is clear also that
what Jesus was to them, unformulated as it was, could not
be annulled even by the tragedy of His fate. Nor would
they have wished it to be annulled, otherwise His fate
could not have become the kind of problem it was. And
what He was to them they did not realise then and
there but only in time, after His death—a common
experience.

Unless it is felt necessary to infer that in Himself He

became something quite different to them from what He had been in the days of His flesh (and how is this possible?), it is sufficient to maintain that what happened was the conscious and explicit formulation of a conviction which arose directly out of what He had always been to them. A kind of objectivity may be necessary to the expression of this experience: it is not necessary to the experience itself.

It is possible to reject the circumstantial stories in which the conviction that created the Church is incapsulated, without rejecting the conviction. But is it possible to find a halfway house between objectivity and subjectivity? Is there anything called semi-objectivity? Is there an appearance which is not physical? If there were, would not this be the same thing under a different name, felt to be necessary for the same reasons as the physical?

A crisis of conviction may be of such a nature as to require expression in objective terms in order to be communicable. It may involve what the experiencer genuinely believes to be objective factors. The point at issue however is whether one considers an appearance of some kind necessary as of the essence of the experience or whether the essential in the experience is the new conviction. In the former case objectivity is imperative; in the latter it is at best contingent.

If we survey two of the most signal instances of a crisis of conviction in Scripture, that of Isaiah and that of Paul, no one thinks the experience less valid if it is regarded as personal and subjective. It is not required that we should believe that others present in the Temple at the same time as Isaiah would have seen what he saw. It is stated that Paul's companions did not.

True objectivity in these instances is therefore not regarded as essential. The question arises whether the "objectivity" which the participants reported was the agency and essence of the crisis or simply its concomitant. No one would assert that such a crisis of experience in no way depended on the concurrent life of the participant.

CHAPTER SEVENTEEN

THE EMPHASIS ON INSTRUCTION

REFLECTION on the contents of the Gospels will show that the question dominating the minds of the Evangelists was that of the Person of Christ. It might be said that they wrote to raise and answer the question: Who or what is Jesus? This is the *esse* of Christian preaching, the nucleus of the cell of evangelism. It predetermines the content of Christian worship and Christian ethics. It prescribes that Christianity shall not be only a cult or a system of morality but a faith.

In Mark the question is raised in one way or another, often in the form of a direct question, by John the Baptist, the disciples, the demoniacs, the Pharisees, the official representatives of Church and state. The identity of Jesus is the basis of the Birth-narratives in Matthew and Luke. Jesus appears to be a babe in a manger, but in reality He is the King of the Jews, the Saviour of the world. This is the theme of the Fourth Gospel also, not only in the Prologue but throughout, and pointedly in the series of "I am" sayings.

That speculation on the question, Who is Jesus? began in His lifetime it is impossible to doubt. His words and works compelled it. In the eyes of the Evangelists they are specially important because they are evidence which leads to the answer. "Go and tell John what things ye have seen and heard" (Luke 7:22). In all probability the question was raised first and in its simplest form in His own home town. When a man surpasses expectations, no one is more surprised than the people of his own locality.

But it reached more considerable proportions as His reputation grew. He was accounted a prophet. More than a prophet? If so, how much more and what more? His fame increased. His life became the focus of rumour and speculation as He grew to the stature of a national figure in the eyes of His contemporaries. This was inevitable but there are many indications that it was not welcome.

The crisis for this speculation on the identity of Jesus, as for almost everything in the total Christian event, is the crucifixion. From that point the question has to be asked and answered (if it is still considered important) in the light of the knowledge that He died like a criminal, if not as a criminal. The Cross is the touchstone. All that went before leads up to it; all that follows descends from it. It may be a climax of defeat and disappointment or worse; it may be a climax of vindication and glory. Which it is depends on who He is.

To the populace, to Pilate, to the Sanhedrin, the crucifixion of Jesus was the answer, final and irrevocable, that made the question no longer significant. That Jesus could be crucified was sufficient to convince the Jewish leaders that He had been an imposter. Whatever estimate Pilate made of Him, it was not high enough to forbid His being treated as a criminal. In the eyes of the people the Cross was the end, whether they regretted it or not. For all these the incident was closed. But not for some of His disciples. For them the question was still a very live issue. It had not been answered even yet and it was more urgent than ever.

We noted as one of the features of the post-crucifixion narratives, the emphasis on instruction by the Risen Christ. On what does this instruction centre? On the

necessity, the inevitability, of the Cross and the consequences that flow from it. This surely means that the
interest of the disciples converges from both sides on
the crucifixion of Jesus. This is so because the Cross is
the key to His identity and His identity is the question
that will not let them go.

Now until this seemingly incongruous happening, the
crucifixion of Jesus, is seen as something necessary to the
destiny of Jesus, there can be no answer to the question of
His identity. He can remain a prophet, but if He is more
than a prophet, the Cross must be more than His martyrdom; it must be seen as inseparable from His divinely
ordained role—however that role is to be described.

This profound riddle was solved. The disciples had
a Gospel on the other side of the crucifixion simply because it was solved. But it was not solved and could not
have been solved before the crucifixion. The bewilderment with which the whole question of the identity of
Jesus is encompassed in the Gospel records is due to
a simple fact—the ante-dating of the solution.

After the riddle was solved, the Gospel was com-
pounded of that solution and the Gospels, inevitably,
were written in the light of it. The effect was to project
the solution into the pre-crucifixion era when, as a matter
of history, the solution was not known. The story of
Jesus is told by the light of an answer which could not
have been known at the time of the events recorded.

Thus the story is folded back on itself so that what was
known later is supposed to have been known at a previous
stage. The faith of the evangelists makes an anachronistic
leap which was certain to distort the history. This ante-
dating of the answer causes disconcerting out-cropping of
the post-crucifixion data within the pre-crucifixion story.
In the Fourth Gospel where the evangelist frankly begins

with his conclusion, the whole story is re-phrased in the light of this conclusion. In the Synoptic Gospels also the presentation is modified but to a lesser degree. The intrusion of post-crucifixion influence is therefore more obvious.

There are two fundamental matters that are raised by scholars who approach the subject of the life of Jesus from quite a different angle from our own. They are raised because of awareness of the difficulty of accepting them as and where they occur in the Gospel record. The first concerns the Messianic title and the second concerns the forecasts of the resurrection.

Many scholars find it difficult to believe that Jesus claimed to be Messiah. The Gospels time and again represent Him as silencing any claim made by others on His behalf. At the same time it is obvious the Gospel writers fully believe that the title rightly belongs to Him. But if He was Messiah, why did He not "tell them plainly"?

Those who take the records as they stand are bound to find this a baffling conundrum. The truth is, the question is being asked and answered when as yet it was not clearly formulated and could not have been answered at all. To the bewilderment arising from the Evangelists' understandable predisposition to write history in the light of faith are added the sophisticated attempts of commentators to solve a historical problem by means of theological jugglery.

If the records are taken at their face value, it is impossible to escape frustrating contradictions. These arise because of the supposed necessity to claim that Jesus both was and professed to be the Messiah, and this in face of obvious indications in the records that the question had not yet presented itself in this particular form.

The usual exegesis of the difficulty is to regard as fixed

the proposition that He was and claimed to be Messiah and to proceed to explain away anything to the contrary. This is done by surmising that the title in the mind of Jesus bore a completely different connotation from that which it bore in the minds of all His contemporaries, including His disciples. He was the Messiah, but not their Messiah. Thus He could not accept their use of the title and they could not know His. Hence He could neither accept nor reject the title. Only when a few of His disciples were re-educated in the true meaning of it could He welcome it.

This is surely a rather over-subtle piece of rationalisation. To accept a designation only on condition that it can be evacuated of its present content and refashioned in a different image is anything but a plain and open proceeding; to live with such ambiguity at the core of one's being requires a kind of ambivalence which nobody associates with the mind of Jesus.

To use Messiah to convert Messiah, to cast out Satan by Satan, to conceive a new idea but dress it in a garb which makes it indistinguishable from that which it would replace, is not a programme for One whose virtue as the greatest teacher is simple direct utterance from the heart to the heart. Such a recondite scheme has no place in the pre-crucifixion period.

If the only contemporary meaning of Messiah was so alien to the mind of Jesus as is presupposed, why use it at all? What compulsion was there? New wine should be poured into new wineskins.

And is Jesus to be regarded as One who cared about names and titles to this extent? He who warned His hearers against saying, "Lord, Lord" was quite as likely to have warned them against saying, "Messiah, Messiah", if necessary.

Here is nothing but radical incompatibility, a tailored theory which neither haps nor hides. It is an attempt to do not only the impossible but the unnecessary. It arises because dogma has overpowered history and entered into unlawful possession.

Because the question of Jesus' identity became all-important to the Church and therefore to the Evangelists, it is imagined that this question, in the same form, was equally important to Jesus in the days of His flesh. Because the Church's and the Evangelists' answer to the question was "Messiah, but not Jewish Messiah", it is imagined that this must have been Jesus' understanding of the matter also. When we realise that the question and the answer are both antedated, the sophistries of the commentators are seen for what they are.

Incidentally, this kind of problem does not arise in the Fourth Gospel for the simple reason that this Evangelist has cut the Gordian knot. He starts with a Jesus who is Logos, Son, Messiah, a Jesus moreover who, in His lifetime, asks a verdict on His own designation as a matter of eternal consequence. He is plainly and openly who He is; men must either acknowledge or deny: there is no dubiety.

Now this is the position of the missionary Church. But who would claim that it represents the historical situation in the pre-crucifixion period? The Fourth Gospel solves the problem before it begins its narrative. The Synoptics are snarled up in it in the midst of their narrative. But in fact the question and answer in their urgent form were not present till after the narrative reached its conclusion. The faith of the Church about Jesus was understandably read back into the days of Jesus' ministry. But there it cannot find a congruous historical setting.

We turn now to the second matter about which scholars have been doubtful for a long time, the prophecies in the Gospels specifically referring to the resurrection of Jesus. These are in quite a different case from either the forecasts of His death or the apocalyptic utterances regarding the end of the age. The fate of the true prophet in Israel is well defined and the execution of John the Baptist was more than a recent memory. That Jesus should be aware He was treading a path which traditionally led to rejection and death, and should say so in so many words to His disciples, is surely not to be wondered at.

Again, no prophet in the true tradition had failed to speak of the terrors and promises awaiting at the end of the age. This was one of the main reasons why he was a prophet at all. It gave point and urgency to the word of the Lord he was commissioned to utter. That Jesus was certainly a prophet, whatever more He was, and spoke of the imminence of the end, is generally accepted, though how far this influenced His teaching is still debated.

But no prophet rose from the dead or foretold that he would.

Some scholars who reject such a prophecy on Jesus' part have argued that, if Jesus knew and foretold that He would rise from the dead, this foreknowledge would make the crucifixion nothing more than a masque. The Cross is robbed of its profoundest quality and reduced to triviality. There is great force in this reasoning, but it is the approach of the theologian, not the historian.

The reason why the forecasts of resurrection are suspect may not be based on the limitation of Jesus' knowledge or the effects of the forecasts on the doctrine of the Person of Christ or the doctrine of Redemption. They are based simply on the impossibility of reconciling such forecasts with the main features of the story.

Mark records that on three separate occasions Jesus warned His disciples of His approaching death and consequent resurrection. There is every evidence that the disciples received and accepted the forecast of death and acted precisely as might be expected in view of it. There is no evidence that they received and accepted a forecast of resurrection, and every evidence that they did not act then or later in accordance with such an expectation.

Again, and even more clearly, the story has been folded back upon itself. It is told in the light of what the Church believed about the death and resurrection of Jesus who was to them undoubtedly the Messiah. It is impossible to conceive that the disciples should have been told in advance of such a staggering event as the resurrection of their Master and not only should not have believed it, but should have forgotten they had ever been told. It is easier to believe they might have forgotten most of what Jesus ever said, than to credit that this unprecedented secret should have dropped out of memory without trace.

If, then, we accept these two propositions, that Jesus did not accept the Messianic title and did not forecast His bodily resurrection, this means that the disciples come to the post-crucifixion period without any assurance about His Messiahship and without any expectation that the Cross will not have been the end of the life of Jesus. This is to say that when Jesus died they were left to wonder who He had been and why He had died. His person and His death are together one enigma.

If we now examine the teaching in the post-crucifixion narratives, these two features are prominent. Jesus spoke to them about Himself. Jesus spoke to them about the necessity of His death. These are precisely the matters on which they required enlightenment if they were to continue to stand apart from the judgment of the populace, Pilate and Caiaphas, that is to say if they were to believe and become a Church.

It is now time to notice that the one thing that could satisfy the disciples on these counts, the one thing which could at once reverse the obvious consequences of Jesus' crucifixion and answer the question as to His identity, was the conviction that He is the Messiah, a conviction arrived at in full view of the Cross.

Here if anywhere is the birthplace of the Christian faith. We may be able to be more precise but it is certain that no Church is possible after the crucifixion until the conviction that He who had lived with the disciples, bound them to Himself by a covenant and died for them was none other than God's Messiah. This was revelation beyond all expectation and, indeed, scarcely to be adequately expressed except in terms belonging to a New Age.

The additional topics of teaching mentioned in our records are worth attention. There is first of all the future of the movement. They were instructed regarding the Kingdom of God and the plan for them as witnesses, says Luke–Acts. They were commissioned to carry the Gospel into all the world, says Matthew. They were given the Holy Spirit with a divine commission, says John.

This is the point at which they found it possible to think and plan in terms of a new and radical movement in which the aims and ideals of Jesus would go on into the future. They recognise themselves now to be the chosen associates of the Messiah through whom His work and purpose will be brought to its true fruition. This is the faith that made and sustained the Church.

The other notable factor in the narratives is the association of definite persons with the initial event. They are a small company at the beginning. Even so, our traditions are very sparing in their references to specific people. Our writers are looking down a long corridor of time. It is not very easy to detect who is there and what they are saying and doing at the very beginning. The birth of the Church is like the birth of a great man. Nobody knows what he will become and by the time he is universally recognised everybody who ever knew him has died or forgotten, if they ever knew, what he was like as a child and what he did and said when he was a boy.

It was not to be known what the future of the Church would be, and certain that none could then have the least conception of its destiny. So much that we would like to know is for ever lost. Only when those who had been present were no longer alive and able to pass on by word of mouth the story of the beginnings out of their own experience was the need for a record fully appreciated. And then too much had sunk beyond the horizon never to come into view again.

But one figure has imprinted his memory on all the pages that have come down to us. And the picture we have of him is clearer than that of any other. Some are mere names; others appear for a moment and then are lost for ever. But Simon Peter is there at the heart of it all from the first. Why? Is it simply because he was the first to be called by Jesus at the Lake of Galilee? Is it only because he is a colourful, impetuous character?

These facts alone can scarcely account for the prominence of Peter in the records of the Church, in the Gospels, Acts and Epistles. We have singled out as one of the noteworthy features of the post-crucifixion narratives the fact that in every account this man is in the pre-eminent place. Even the Gospel of John gives back-handed witness to this fact. We must now turn our attention to it.

CHAPTER EIGHTEEN

THE PRIMACY OF PETER

In our investigation into the birth of the Christian faith we began from the documents that bear earliest testimony to its existence. We first delimited the time and then the place. Next we examined the event itself to discover its nature.

Our conclusion so far has been that, whatever else may be said about the event which is the birth of the faith, it is inseparable from the conviction that Jesus is the Messiah, a conviction necessarily arrived at after and in spite of the crucifixion of Jesus. This conviction is first private and then public. In its private aspect it is the birth of the faith; in its public aspect it is the birth of the Church. In traditional language these are related to "the third day" and the "Day of Pentecost" respectively.

Is it possible now to go one step further with the help of our documents and point to the first person of whom it was true to say, "He is convinced, in spite of (or even because of) the Cross, that Jesus is Messiah"? The present chapter is concerned with this possibility.

What we have to do with here is a matter of someone's personal assurance, however arrived at. Christianity has been and remains in the first instance a personal commitment. To this day nothing can be conceived as more intimate, individual and personal than a man's faith in Jesus Christ. This is true if we are thinking of Christianity in terms of the New Testament meaning of faith.

That Christianity also has its public aspect is beyond question. But hereditary Christianity which equates being a Christian with being a citizen of a Christian country or having one's name on the roll of a Christian organisation, is not what the New Testament is about. Christianity is what created the Church. What the Church makes of Christianity may be and often has been something very different. Christianity has begun to exist in the world when someone says, "I believe Jesus is the Messiah". It continues for the same kind of reason.

As we have already noticed, all our documents bear witness that if anyone can be identified as the significant person it is Simon Peter. There is no need to recount the various post-crucifixion incidents in which he appears, but they prove beyond all doubt that in this matter Peter's role is pre-eminent. That this is due simply to his being one of the company or to his being a colourful personality is not sufficient explanation. He is described as being there and is revealed as a colourful personality (in the Gospels) simply because of the part he played. He is spotlighted because he is at the centre, not because the light has been moved from the centre to spotlight him.

Now if this is a reasonable assumption, it is likely we shall see traces of it in the Gospel narrative. Since every other aspect of this event has cast its shadow forward into the record of the pre-crucifixion period, it is presumable that this aspect also has done so. The call of Peter as the first disciple may be an indication that this is so, first in time being collated with first in importance.

But immediately this question is raised, what leaps to the mind is the confession of Peter near Caesarea Philippi. An examination of this incident reveals the most pertinent relations with the total event with which we are concerned.

This has always and rightly been regarded as a key

incident. Scholars have been right in the importance they
have attributed to it but wrong in not realising that its
subject is exactly what it purports to be. The result is that
in attempting to find a place for it in the pre-crucifixion
ministry of Jesus (as, indeed, the documents themselves
do), they have never been able to combat the violence it
does to the record of the life of Jesus and the beginning of
the Church.

It is the major cause of the bewilderment which we
noted earlier in regard to the question of Jesus' identity
and the significance of the Cross. In its present position,
it misleads us on these immense issues and creates confusion in certain other directions. In its rightful place, it
is supremely congruous to its own subject matter and also
throws light on other matters which in its present context
it only serves to obscure.

As an instance of the confusion which displacement has
caused, let us consider the effect of this incident in its
present place on the story of Peter's denial of Jesus.

We are required to believe that Peter's denial of any
association with Jesus takes place in spite of his conviction that He is none other than the Messiah. This is
utterly incomprehensible. It makes the incident a repudiation of his faith in and any association with God's
anointed. This is the very act of which it is said that he
who does any such thing will be disowned in the sight of
God. Such an act is not simply an instance of moral
cowardice: it is the only true betrayal of Messiah. It is the
ultimate rejection.

But the record by itself (i.e. not read in the deflected
light of the confession story) is simply an account of moral
failure at the point of extreme pressure. It is a failure of
nerve, not the betrayal of a sacred assurance on which a
man's eternal destiny may depend.

Had it been otherwise, Peter had more reason to de-spair than Judas. Indeed, they must exchange places. Judas betrayed the whereabouts of Jesus but Peter denied the Messiah. If, as some think, what Judas betrayed was the Messianic secret, then he is damned for affirming that Jesus is Messiah while Peter is pardoned for denying it!

In the post-crucifixion period the same circumstances reveal a very different Peter. The reason is plain. He now holds a conviction about Jesus that he would rather die than surrender. Now he is sure Jesus is Messiah; before the crucifixion he had no such certainty.

This illustration shows that the confession incident is displaced by making clear that the result of forcing it into its present position in the narrative is to make nonsense of other incidents which appear to have no direct relation to it.

We have previously noted that references to the iden-tity of Jesus as Messiah and prophecies of resurrection are antedated. This incident contains both. Thus, on two different counts, the incident is palpably misplaced and obviously belongs to the period with which we are pri-marily concerned. It is post-crucifixion narrative.

The difficulties of commentators in treating the con-fession incident are eloquent in the same sense. They mostly recognise that the confession of Peter is of the utmost importance, but at the same time they are aware of the grave difficulties it raises. It is too significant to be overlooked, yet the consequences of accepting it in its present setting are confusion. The result is what might be expected and can be seen in most commentaries.

Particularly is this so with the Matthew version. Here there are additions which must be regarded by such com-mentators as later interpolations, as for instance when Jesus is said to speak of the Church in precise terms. The usual explanation is that this is an intrusion made by the Church in order to give the prestige and authority to the Church which such a reference upon the lips of Jesus Himself could confer. The Church was founded by Christ. It is not unnatural to imagine that He should have referred to its foundations. To say that He did so is no great harm. It is true in spirit, if not in fact. Only the historian is interested in such nice distinctions.

But this will not do. The necessity for such an interpretation arises for one reason only—because the incident is misplaced. The fact is that this confession incident is a true tradition which relates precisely to the subject with which it deals, the birth of the faith, and to the time at which the subject became relevant, the post-crucifixion period.

The reference to the Church did not need to be intruded. It was the very subject of the whole incident. Not that we can take it as it stands even when it is transposed to its rightful place. But if we remove it to its true position, it is perfectly congruent with other material belonging to the same circumstances. It no longer creates confusion in regard to other apparently unrelated incidents.

It is now time to consider the confession incident itself. We see that everything in it points to the fact that here we have an event which may be second in significance only to the Cross itself. This incident points us directly to the place, the time and the person, the total object of our search. Every aspect of the incident leads straight to our goal. It is in itself in summary the story of the birth of the faith. It is far more illuminating than the story of the Transfiguration, which many are quite ready to transpose as a post-crucifixion narrative. And it is much more obviously a post-crucifixion narrative than the

Transfiguration, although there is no difficulty in accepting the transposition of the latter.

The subjects we have been forced to find at the heart of the crucial interval are the question of the identity of Jesus, the mystery of the Cross, the birth of a conviction in which both find a common answer, namely, that Jesus is Messiah. These are the presuppositions of the faith that created the Church. Without them what we may call the incident of Jesus is at an end, as it was for everyone except the disciples and until the Church was born. Now the Synoptic records of the Petrine confession bring together and unite them in one incident.

(It is noteworthy that the Fourth Gospel has no need of such a precise incident. It begins by assuming this union as made in Heaven. Jesus is never anything less than Messiah from the beginning; the Cross is His glorification known in advance. Andrew divines the truth from the first (1:41). Peter reiterates what they all know (6:69). In the Fourth Gospel doubt is due to spiritual obtuseness, not to mental uncertainty. Since it is primarily theological and only incidentally historical, the Fourth Gospel provides for no evolution, no gradual unfolding and gradual realisation, only existence and the correlatives of knowledge and ignorance. But even in the Fourth Gospel Peter is inseparably associated with the confession of Messiahship. Incidentally, if we acknowledge that here the confession of Jesus as Messiah is antedated to the very beginning of the Gospel story, is there any reason to deny that it could be anachronic in the Synoptics also? The Synoptics show us history modified by theology: the Fourth Gospel shows us theology modifying history.)

The identity of the historical Jesus is a riddle, the Cross is a bewildering tragedy to His followers and the initial discovery of the fact which unites and resolves them both takes place in the mind of one man and explains the existence of the Church.

This is precisely the subject matter of the passage we are now considering. The incident opens with the dominating question, Who is Jesus? The answers hitherto given are inadequate. The true, that is to say, the resolving, answer is given by Peter, with the acquiescence of the other disciples. Immediately associated with this is the second crucial question which is the crucifixion.

It is evident that this is a record of mental and spiritual conflict upon the two key themes that lie at the foundation of the Church. If He is the Christ, why the crucifixion? If He has been crucified, can He be the Christ? This is the dilemma of the post-crucifixion period, a dilemma which existed for those who had followed Jesus, loved Him but never understood Him, a dilemma which they could not simply abandon because their love of Him and His love of them was stronger than death.

The addition to the record of Mark which we find in Matthew's Gospel is not an intrusion but an interpretative comment. It is proof that this staggering confession first uttered by Peter was recognised as the birth of the faith and therefore the birth of the Church. It specifically states that the Church is founded on the confession of Peter and thereby tells us that this is what was believed at the time the Gospel was written. If we ask why this was believed and for how long it had been believed, there seems no good reason to answer otherwise than that it was true and had been considered true from the start.

There are two interesting sidelights. The first is the reference to Satan and the comment which charges Peter with thinking as other men think and not as God thinks. Nothing could more plainly indicate that we are here in

the presence of the kind of situation which we have in the
Temptation of Jesus. The reference to Satan and to the
will of God as the only valid choice enforce the parallel.
This is the record of an inward conflict, presumably in
the mind of Peter. What men have thought is that Jesus
was a prophet but is now dead and therefore can't have
been Messiah. Is Peter satisfied that this is so? The confession is the answer. Because the whole incident has been
misplaced, the answer has been given before the question
is stated.

The second is in the Matthew version. The blessing
of Peter is consequent on his confession that Jesus is
Messiah. But it is made clear that this conviction of
Jesus' Messiahship did not arise in the mind of Peter
because of any objective phenomenon—"Flesh and blood
hath not revealed it unto thee." If this incident is transposed, then the significance of this comment is very
profound and of such a character as to vindicate anew
what has been said in a previous chapter regarding the
accounts of post-crucifixion appearances.

Our conclusion therefore is that the faith whose birth
we have sought to trace takes its rise in the mind of Peter.
He is thus truly regarded as the rock on which the Church
is founded in virtue of his confession that Jesus is Messiah.
This accounts for the reverence in which he was held by
the Church and the prominence he enjoys in the Gospel
narratives. He may not have been alone in the conviction
for long, but to him goes the honour of being the first to
achieve and express it and nothing can rob him of this
singular privilege.

Tu es Petrus is certainly a text to conjure with. But let
the conjurer beware of mistaking the nature of its power.
It is a text of faith, not of dogma. Here the lamp of faith is
lit but it must be set on a lampstand, not under a bushel.

NOTE ON THE POSITION OF THE CAESAREA PHILIPPI INCIDENT

QUESTIONS about order in Mark seem to have arisen almost on publication, as the famous quotation from Eusebius shows. What Papias and the Presbyter meant by "not in order" is not clear. It tends to be interpreted in the light of the interpreter's own view of the Gospel.

In recent years the text of the New Testament has been subjected to scientific analysis. Modern statistical techniques make it possible to state the characteristic features of Gospels and Epistles.

In their book *The Structure of the Fourth Gospel* (Oliver & Boyd, 1961), G. H. C. Macgregor and A. Q. Morton have shown that the structure of John is quite different from that of Galatians, for instance. It may be indicated by saying that an Epistle is composed, a Gospel constructed.

A. Q. Morton in *New Testament Source Analysis* (in preparation) has carried out a general examination of the six major books, i.e. the four Gospels, Acts and Revelation. He shows there are two features of the Gospels as a whole, and of Mark in particular, which remove many of the supposed difficulties in the way of regarding the Transfiguration and Caesarea Philippi as post-crucifixion stories.

1. The Gospels are not orderly arrangements of narratives. They are aggregations of large blocks of material. It is therefore dangerous to apply chronological tests to any single story.

Morton demonstrates that the Passion Narrative in all Four Gospels is so uniform and consistent in sequence that all four must have a common ancestry. The whole Passion sequence must be regarded as a unit.

Papias' remark therefore cannot refer to individual stories but to these blocks. If these are not in order then the chronology is in very sketchy condition.

Mark begins with the Baptism and ends with the Passion narrative which concludes the ministry. The Transfiguration and Caesarea Philippi immediately precede the final block. They are not public but private events and their position in the Gospel says nothing as to their true chronological position.

2. The second argument from the structure of the Gospel is fully illustrated in *The Structure of the Fourth Gospel*. There Morton examines the prose of composite works. One feature is a much higher proportion of long paragraphs. He gives the rule that, of all paragraphs longer than twice the average length of paragraph in the Gospel, over 80 per cent are discrete sources which have been copied into the book or made up from source material.

Mark has seven such paragraphs—The Gadarene Swine, the Beheading of John the Baptist, the Feeding of the Multitude, On Cleanliness, Caesarea Philippi, the Boy Epileptic, Peter's Denial. Mathematical probability indicates that four-fifths of these are copied from sources.

A narrative like Caesarea Philippi is therefore more likely than not to be copied from a source and the structure of the whole Gospel is such as to indicate that an insertion of this kind is not made in chronological order.

The author is not competent to expound what is obviously a highly technical statistical argument. What he suggests, with the concurrence of Morton who has been consulted on the point, is that the structure of Mark does not imply that the Caesarea Philippi incident is in its correct chronological order. Its present position is no handicap to an argument which aims to set it in its true position.

In conclusion, it is worth considering whether the tradition of disorder in Mark would have been handed down initially if all it referred to was misplacement of incidents within the middle section of the Gospel. It is much more certain to have been considered important if it was thought that one or more incidents included in the middle section ought to appear after the Passion Narrative.

PART IV

ORTHODOXY AND MODERN CRITICISM

CHAPTER NINETEEN

"RESURRECTIONEM CARNIS"

WHAT the documents belonging to the earliest stage of Christianity reveal is the buoyancy and ebullience of a new faith. This is particularly true of the Pauline letters, the Synoptic Gospels and the Acts of the Apostles. The later New Testament writings such as the Pastoral Epistles, 2 Peter and Jude already show signs of a descent into the mediocrity of thought and feeling which many post-apostolic and patristic writings display. These later works disclose a faith which has outlived its pristine exuberance and is adjusting itself to a different era. It continues potent and active but less spontaneous, less lyrical. It is stated or dictated rather than sung.

What happens when a faith survives into a different era from that in which it was born? Is it the same faith? These are ambiguous questions, as if one should ask whether the man of fifty is the same man. The same as what? By many criteria the grown man is not the same as the growing boy. But he is identifiable as now "this" which then was "that" and in his own consciousness he says, "I am he". Whether we are impressed by the aspect of identity or by the aspect of difference depends on our purpose in making the comparison. Can we, however, use such an analogy here?

In the case of Christianity, as indeed of any religious faith, it is often assumed that the same initial endowment which created the new faith persists into history, producing the same kind or quality of religious life in generation after generation. In this resides the element of identity, the constant which persists whatever variations supervene in the course of time.

This is sometimes set out as an identity of faith accompanied by development of theology, unity of experience with continuity of expression. It is analogous to the "preformation" type of evolutionary theory in which the embryo is endowed with all the parts and members of the full grown organism. Doctrinal development is regarded simply as the explication of the body of doctrine divinely delivered at the beginning.

But identity of one faith in two different ages is as elusive as the identity of the man of fifty with the boy. Something there is which allows us in certain circumstances to say, "This was that", but whether this something is itself a constant is not evident and the difference between the two is not to be overlooked.

The epigenetic conception of development seems more appropriate here as in biology. The organism is not simply an expansion or enlargement of the original datum. It is a product of the changing relationship between the germ and its environment and the process of assimilation from the changing environment.

But this is not the usual account that Christianity gives of itself. In the period when definition of the faith was necessary as a canon of orthodoxy and an instrument for the detection of heresy, it fastened upon theological expression as the constant element and made creed the guarantor of continuity. Novelty and deviation were the marks of heresy. This view is implied in the 5th century Vincentian Canon which states that the truth of the Church is what has been believed always, everywhere and by all Christians—*quod ubique, quod semper, quod ab*

omnibus creditum est. This is how the Church thought of
its essence and history; it is how many people think of it
today.

But in simple fact Christianity survived to have a
history through the centuries precisely because this was
not the case. It was because it was able to find new and
apposite theological and intellectual expression with great
facility in the first four centuries that it attained superiority. From the historical point of view it survived because
it did not remain the same. It modified its theology, its
ethics, and its organisation profoundly in passing from
the milieu of 1st-century Palestine to the more complex
environment of the Roman Empire.

To survive, the Church needed to preserve its identity,
to be the one true Church. It required also to express itself in terms adequate to the thought and need of changing times. These twin ideas of identity and adequacy
are constantly in tension, especially as intellectual expression is increasingly regarded as the criterion of the
faith. If the faith is regarded as having been once delivered to the saints at the beginning, the question is how
it can be expressed in new language without running the
risk of modification and even falsification. How to con-
serve both identity and adequacy? It is doubtful whether
on these terms it is ever possible.

In each new age and environment Christians felt
bound to cling as long as possible to the terms in which
Christianity had expressed itself in the New Testament
period. An interesting instance is found in the objections
made to the use of "homoousion" (of the same substance),
in reference to the relation between the Son and the
Father, during the Christological controversies of the 5th
century. The term was used by Athanasius and became
the touchstone of orthodoxy. But many condemned it at

first on the ground that it was unscriptural and therefore unsuited for a creed.*

Here the question whether a new expression of the faith is or is not acceptable is bound up with the question whether a new expression need or need not affect the essence of the faith. The tension between identity and adequacy in such a setting can be reduced only by general agreement to regard one expression of the faith as both true and adequate, both now and in the future. This was the function to be performed by the ideal creed.

The historian is more aware of change than identity and indeed the hope of proving identity is a forlorn one. What was believed about Jesus by His contemporaries, by Paul, by the author of the Prologue to the Fourth Gospel, by the Council of Nicaea, is not seen to be precisely the same thing in different words. The subject is nominally the same but is it in fact? The conclusions are palpably different. If it is argued that the latest belief is the completest understanding of the earliest, this is still something short of identity.

Both the environment and the content of a historical faith do in fact undergo some translation in the course of time. If we call it development, this in itself tells us nothing, unless we adopt the deterministic theory of evolution indicated above which posits inevitable progress in powers of interpretation as a historical necessity.

But this in turn cuts at the roots of the possibility of a definition of the faith which is valid beyond its own period. Unless we deny that a faith is obliged to be concerned with truth, the fact that nothing is true simply because it has been believed is fatal to this position. We

---

* Cf. J. F. Bethune-Baker, *An Introduction to the Early History of Christian Doctrine*, p. 171.

have thus departed radically from the idea of identity as a historical description of Christianity.

Over and above all this, it is doubtful whether we can assume without further ado that the content of a faith can be treated as an organism which develops while remaining essentially the same. The analogical use of the notion of organism is evident. But a faith is not in any appreciable sense a body of some kind which has a parasitic existence in one set of believers after another. What men believe is related to what other men have believed by a process of assimilation and not by consciously directed invasion of their personality by some entity to be identified as the organism of a faith. In such a process there is no guarantee or even possibility of identical transmission since the present is not simply the past at a different time.

Once the faith is reduced to a formula which becomes a criterion of orthodoxy, the same form of words will give the illusion of identity and may indeed impose the imprint of identity as far as a changing environment will allow. But the problem of holding in tension the ideas of identity of essence and adequacy of expression remains. It is set for each new generation. To destroy this tension is to cut the thread of life. Securing identity at the cost of modernity leads to ossification of primitive belief. Modernity regardless of identity produces a new entity. What in fact happens is something of both, which the notions of organism and development are not able to accommodate.

Christianity began in an environment of increasing hostility to Judaism and developed in the early centuries in one of increasing hostility to Gnosticism. In both cases the belief in resurrection was one of the tenets which drew the fire of opponents and merited the deliberate defence of believers. Once the faith enters that area

where assertion is no longer primary and apologetic becomes a foremost necessity, the very act of concentration
on particular doctrines initiates an alteration in expression
or at least in emphasis.

We have seen how the delay in the Parousia created
difficulty from the beginning. The more it was extended,
the more necessary was an adjustment in the statement of
belief about it, to cope with the postponement of the
things of the end. The immediate prospect of the
Parousia fades and resurrection is relegated to the end of
the world.

When we come to the belief in the resurrection of Jesus
the change is inevitably in the direction of increasing
insistence on the historicity, factuality and corporeality
of the resurrection. This process goes to its limit.
Orthodoxy ultimately has to express itself as far as belief
in resurrection is concerned in the uncompromising words
"resurrectionem carnis", the resurrection of the flesh, not
"corporis" (body) as in Paul.

If Paul had been able to read and accept the last chapters of the canonical Gospels, he would not have been so
insistent that flesh and blood (*sarx kai haima*) cannot inherit the kingdom of God (1 Cor. 15:50). The belief
that the risen Jesus had flesh and bones (*sarka kai ostea*,
Luke 24:39) stands in contrast to the view that we must
be changed (*allagesometha*, 1 Cor. 15:51), and that the
resurrection body is quite different from the body of
flesh. "Paul believes in the resurrection of the *body*, not
of the *flesh*. The flesh is the power of death, which must
be destroyed."*

The Pauline compromise between Hebrew and Greek
anthropology was unfitted to withstand the attacks of a

* O. Cullmann, *Immortality of the Soul or Resurrection of the Dead?* p.
46.

Judaism which demanded credible evidence that Jesus was truly raised from the dead, that the resurrection faith was based on historical event.* The post-crucifixion narratives of the Gospels proffer evidence that here is no ghost, hallucination or idle tale but act and fact. They are the first and decisive step on the way to the doctrine of the resurrection of the flesh.

The pressure in this direction continued after the conflict with Judaism had resulted in complete separation and undying hostility. The struggle against Gnosticism necessitated the same kind of insistence on the historicity and bodily reality of the resurrection.

This syncretistic religious philosophy flourished along with Christianity for about three hundred years. It offered means of expressing some Christian beliefs in terms which were congenial and so more adequate to the times. The later books of the New Testament show that already to some extent Gnostic modes of expression have been adopted and already there is awareness of the potential danger of Gnosticism—a love–hate relationship.

The Gnostic doctrine that the flesh is essentially evil and that the redeemer of man is spirit and not flesh can be countered only by insistence that redemption is the salvation of the complete man, body and spirit, by a redeemer who is both body and spirit. Thus again the emphasis for apologetic purposes is on the reality of the body of Jesus and of His bodily (fleshly) resurrection. This is consequently incorporated in the great creeds of the Church and becomes one of the things most surely believed by Christians for the next 1500 years.

It may be useful to give some quotations from the fathers to show their understanding of the doctrine.

* Cf. C. G. Montefiore, *Synoptic Gospels*, Vol. 1, p. 405.

Clement of Rome (*c.* 95), after repeating the legend of the phoenix, continues:

"Do we then think it a great marvel if the Creator of the universe is to effect the resurrection of those who served him in holiness with the confidence of a good faith, seeing that he shows us the magnificence of his promise even in a bird?" (*Epis. to Corinth.* xxvi.)

Ignatius (martyred *c.* 115): "For I know and believe that even after his resurrection he was in a physical body; and when he came to Peter and his companions . . . they touched him and believed, when they had contact with his flesh and blood" (*Smyr.* iii).

Irenaeus (*c.* 130–200): "It is clear that the souls of his disciples, for whom the Lord had performed this (i.e. his death and resurrection) will depart to an unseen region, set apart for them by God, and will dwell there until the resurrection which they await. Then they will receive their bodies and will arise entire, that is, in bodily form as the Lord arose, and thus will come into the presence of God" (*Adv. Haer.*, 5, xxxi, 2).

"What is restored to life is not something other than that which dies" (5, xii, 3).

"If God gave existence, when he so willed, to those who did not exist, much more will he restore those who have come into being to the life which He gave them, if He so wills" (5, iii, 2).

Tertullian (*c.* 200): "And so the flesh rises again, in its entirety, in its identity, in its integrity. Wherever it is, it is in safe keeping with God through the most faithful mediator between God and man, Jesus Christ, who will restore God to man and man to God, the spirit to the flesh and the flesh to the spirit" (*De Res. Carnis*, 63).

In his *De Spectaculis*, Tertullian rejoices in the prospect of seeing the famous and successful of this world "groaning now in the lowest darkness . . . tossing in the fiery billows". *Augustine* teaches that the fire of Gehenna is a material flame and that the lost will be furnished with bodies able, like the salamander, to live for ever in the furnace. *Jerome* believed that there would be a restoration of the bones, veins, nerves, teeth and hair at the resurrection.

Those who followed the Pauline teaching in 1 Cor. appear to have been few and far between and were repudiated by the orthodox Church. Thus *Marcion* (died *c.* 160), whose doctrine of Christ was docetic and who was vigorously attacked as a heretic in his own lifetime. Of him *Irenaeus* writes: "And then he says that salvation will be of our souls only, of those souls who have learned his teaching; the body, because forsooth it is taken from the earth, cannot partake in salvation" (*Adv. Haer.*, 1, xxvii, 2).

The great scholar and writer *Origen* (185–254), who succeeded Clement as head of the school of Alexandria, was attacked for his views during his lifetime, and his teaching, under the name of origenism, was condemned by the Council of Alexandria in 400. He held that the resurrection would involve a change from corruptible to incorruptible body as in Paul. "How can men suppose that our animal body is to be changed by the grace of the resurrection and become spiritual? . . . By the command of God the body which was earthly and animal will be replaced by a spiritual body . . . even for those destined for eternal fire or punishment, there will be an incorruptible body through the change of the resurrection" (*De Princ.*, 2, x, 3).

By means of the great creeds the Church reached that consensus of agreement by which the tension between the urge to preserve identity and the need to find adequate means of expression was reduced. It was taken for granted thereafter that Christianity was that which was signified in the acceptance of the Church's creed.

There had never been any major controversy on the specific matter of resurrection. There was general agreement on the statement that Christ rose on the third day and that believers expected their own resurrection. This statement needed neither modification nor elaboration after the resurrection narratives gave it representational form. Once these narratives were generally received as Scripture, nothing further was required. If it was clear that Christ rose in the flesh (and to doubt this was to call in question the sacred narrative), this was the pattern of the resurrection of believers at the end of the world.

Consequently, the teaching of the Church on this particular throughout the centuries till recent times is consistently uniform in essentials, though at different periods the degree of concentration upon the subject varies. A feature of the middle ages, for example, is the obsession with death and the great divide beyond. Lurid descriptions of the awesome events of death and the terrors of the last day, the general resurrection and judgment are the stock-in-trade of all preachers. This is psychologically important for the understanding of the period, but the resurrection idea itself remains what it had been, an event in which the actual body is raised from the grave.

In the mediaeval period the resurrection of Christ does not hold the promise of a new world wherein dwelleth righteousness, or the inspiration to Christian endeavour in this world for the fulfilment of the prayer, "Thy kingdom come!" It is chiefly the assurance to the believer that after his weary travail upon this sin-cursed earth, he will be raised from death like his Lord to enjoy the glory of heaven at the last day.

Forecasts on the delights of heaven and the terrors of hell were general, but the notion of resurrection remained what it had always been from the days of the Gospel narratives. Any speculations on the subject took place within the accepted frame. Thus the popular preacher Olivier Maillard, discussed whether the body of Christ would have decomposed if it had not been for the resurrection. He regarded the subject as "a beautiful theological question".*

The Reformation left untouched the question of the ultimate nature of the doctrine. While the reformers had much to say of the qualifications for participating in the resurrection and of the theological meaning of the resurrection of Jesus in relation to man's redemption, they took over the age-old doctrine without modification. Their attitude to Scripture precluded any other possibility. No one but an unbeliever would wish to question the record or the reality of the event.

We may quote Calvin as representative of the thought of the times in this respect. In dealing with the subject he informs us that "all those things which are invisible to our eyes, or far above the comprehension of our minds, must either be believed on the authority of the oracles of God, or entirely rejected" (*Institutes*, 3, xxv, 5).

On the specific matter of bodily resurrection, he says: "Equally monstrous is the error of those who imagine that souls will not resume the bodies which at present belong to them, but will be furnished with others altogether different . . . Nor is there any point more clearly established in Scripture, than the resurrection of our present bodies . . . If we are to receive new bodies, where will be the conformity between Head and members? Christ rose; was it by making himself a new body? No,

* Cf. J. Huizinga, *The Waning of the Middle Ages*, p. 157.

but according to his prediction, 'Destroy this temple, and in three days I will raise it up'. The mortal body which he before possessed, he again assumed" (3, xxv, 7).

It is when we come to the modern period and the historical method of study as applied to the New Testament and to the growth of religions and institutions, that there appears, not only outside but within the Church, an intellectual barrier to accepting the "*Resurrectionem Carnis*" formula.

CHAPTER TWENTY

TO REASON WHY

IT is not possible to get an adequate idea of the changes that have come about in relation to our subject in the modern period without paying some attention to the general trend of New Testament study and the larger issues of theology. The present chapter notes the difference in climate due to the break-up of what has been called the mediaeval synthesis, i.e. the traditional religious framework within which the life and thought of Western Christendom was carried on. It indicates how the new climate affected men's thoughts about the particular subject of resurrection.

It is possible to speak of modern attitudes to resurrection because the Reformation, the Enlightenment, the explosion of knowledge in the last three hundred years, have destroyed some of the basic assumptions of Western Christendom. In the light of the development of modern freedom of inquiry, the Reformation itself is only a family quarrel within Christianity.

Today the Church, even in nominally Christian countries, is confronted by a secular world which refuses to accept beliefs simply because they have been held for a long time or are backed by ecclesiastical authority. Christian apologetic is required to be much more than a support to traditional belief; it must be a reasoned case which will stand up in face of informed criticism. In these circumstances Christianity has been forced to give up some of the traditional positions as no longer defensible, such as the infallibility of the Scriptures, the historicity of the creation story.

These concessions have not been made in view of sporadic attacks: they are due to a change of climate in thinking, a change which has required the same kind of concessions in other departments of knowledge such as medicine, physics, education, politics.

In his *The Shaping of the Modern Mind* (1953), Crane Brinton states the matter simply: "By the eighteenth century educated men and women, and we may believe many of the uneducated, had come to hold certain beliefs about themselves, about the universe, about what was worth doing on earth, about what could be done on earth, beliefs that their ancestors of the Middle Ages had not held. . . . Much of what the men and women of the eighteenth century and later centuries believed was incompatible with some very important parts of traditional Christian belief" (p. 107).

It is needless to elaborate this statement, but two factors of particular importance to our subject must be noted. One is the new conception of the nature and *modus operandi* of the physical world and the other is the new understanding of history and the method of historical investigation.

These in time resulted in prolonged argument on the nature and possibility of miracle, on the one hand, and the value and use of historical documents on the other. While individual Christian scholars have been in the forefront in these areas of new thinking, the Christian faith has been forced on to the defensive. Butler's *Analogy* (1736) and Paley's *Natural Theology* (1803) are landmarks in the retreat from positions assumed to be impregnable up to and beyond Reformation times.

Christian apologists had taken it as axiomatic that the

miracles of Jesus and in particular His resurrection were irrefutable proof of His uniqueness as Son of God, and that the New Testament was the guarantee that these miracles had taken place. Miracle was the intervention of God in the affairs of nature and the world and needed no argument. All of these positions came under question and the dust of controversy has scarcely settled even yet.

In general it can be said that, while there is no disposition to give up belief in the miraculous, Christianity has been forced to revise its interpretation of "miraculous" and reverse the argument. While it had been common to reason from the miraculous to the uniqueness of Jesus, it now became more common for apologists to use the uniqueness of Jesus as an argument for belief in His miracles. More radical scholars were even prepared to dispense with the miraculous. Thus Harnack in *What is Christianity?* (Eng. trans. 1901) recognised Jesus' moral and religious uniqueness, yet denied that He wrought any miracles in the sense of supernatural acts.

The period of radical historical criticism in the 19th and first half of the 20th century was marked by a relentless questioning of the credibility of the Gospel narratives and the conception of the miraculous. While it is true that there was much extravagance in this period, it is also true that on the whole the retreat from mediaeval attitudes and positions continued. Only in recent years with the rise of what came to be known as Biblical Theology has some respite been devised by theologians and for theologians.

On our specific subject, the traditional view of resurrection as a historical event which is capable of being sustained by historical evidence was bound to become the subject of a new kind of controversy. In it were to be found the twin subjects of miracle and the authority of historical documentation. Since the attitude to both had undergone radical rethinking, the consequences were inevitable.

It is fair criticism of many of the assessments which were made that the underlying assumption was deterministic. It was assumed that the miraculous does not happen; therefore any alleged evidence is false or at least misleading. But, on the other hand, if Christian apologists were determined to maintain that the resurrection was historical event, their apologetic was not serviceable if they could not provide historical substantiation.

In these circumstances many radical critics and some who believed they were serving the best interests of the Church concentrated on providing explanations of the New Testament belief in resurrection which did not require miraculous intervention or which modified the nature or extent of such intervention.

In the case of Strauss and Renan, the rise of belief in the resurrection of Jesus was explained as the result of subjective visions due to the disciples' love for their master and their own excited mental state. Theodor Keim in his *Jesus of Nazara* (1867–72) accepted the subjective explanation but argued that the visions were divinely vouchsafed and provided sufficient evidence that Christ had in fact overcome death, even if His material body was not raised. In this he was followed by B. H. Streeter in *Foundations* (1912).

Perhaps the most scholarly treatment of the subject from the radical historical point of view was Kirsopp Lake's *The Historical Evidence for the Resurrection of Jesus Christ* (1907). Lake supported the subjective thesis. He accounted the story of the empty tomb a case of mistaken identity. Mary went to the wrong tomb and was told, "He is not here". The important addition: "He is risen", was based on a later assumption.

Such works as those mentioned above were often, of course, extravagant both in their assumptions and in their denials, but corporately they are evidence of the insecurity of the traditional attitude to the subject. Lake and Streeter, for instance, were pioneers in this country and their integrity was not in doubt. But they found few who were prepared to follow. The truth is that the general apologetic of the Church was loath to come to terms with the new attitude to miracle and the work of historical criticism. But it was becoming less credible and so less creditable to profess to support a conception of resurrection as historical event, by appeal to documents which were themselves, at the same time, being regarded as the kerygma or preaching of the Church rather than as historical record.

But while this was recognised and admitted elsewhere, as in the question whether it was not now impossible to write a life of Jesus in the grand manner, in the matter of resurrection it was still thought sufficient to restate the old arguments and scout the idea that Christianity's existence could be explained except on the basis of a historical rising from the dead. It was not realised that there is no halfway house between the kind of history which is simply reliance on "authorities" and the history which refuses to regard any single witness as an authority and therefore allows no witness to go unquestioned. Neither was it realised that there is no theological way of maintaining a historical argument, and historical evidence is not interchangeable with theological presupposition.

Meantime the religious climate had changed once again. It was felt that historical criticism had proved disastrous from the point of view of orthodoxy and arid from the point of view of nourishing the church's spiritual life. Moreover, it had raised many questions bearing on the central tenets of the faith, particularly the life, teaching and mission of Jesus, which seemed to have no answer in terms of the traditional theology. The "liberal" movement therefore appeared to be discredited. Since it was associated with fearless and uncommitted investigation of historical issues, the time was ripe for a swing to dogmatic theology.

In the thirties and forties the teaching of Karl Barth was welcomed by many as the answer to the psychological needs of the time. There arose a number of more or less raucous varieties of neo-orthodoxy which had this in common, that they broke off abruptly and disdainfully the dialogue between theology and culture, and took their stand upon what they considered to be an invulnerable esoteric epistemology. The thing to do was to by-pass these unprofitable and insoluble problems raised by overweening human intellect and get through to the supernatural, absolute, irreducible thing itself, the Word of God. If history and mere human reason were intractable, so much the worse for them.

In the setting of the times, there is no denying the *ad hoc* pragmatic service which the "theology of crisis" performed. But at what cost? In 1943 Canon Raven warned that the tendency of the movement was "to set theological over against historical exegesis and, while professing to reject fundamentalism, reproduce its most reactionary characteristics, the contrast between science and religion and between piety and social service".*

In reference to the effects on our conception of Jesus, Raven writes: "To estrange Him from nature and history, to give Him the character of an alien invader, to make of His manhood a disguise and of His temptations a sham fight, this is to empty His revelation of its power to reveal

* *Good News of God*, Hodder & Stoughton, p. 6.

and to reduce His incarnation to the level of previous and mythical theophanies. Unless our theological language is used more exactly and more accurately, the impression that Christianity is a creed outworn will remain and very rapidly increase."*

It is noticeable that during this period a new kind of ambiguity appears in the use of theological language. The theological terminology of the reformers was reinstated; but who could say that the words still meant what they used to mean? Luther, Calvin, Aquinas and Augustine were summoned to the defence of the faith once delivered to the saints by many who professed to have repudiated the mediaeval assumptions on which these doctors of the Church had necessarily built the new theology of their own day.

More than any other, "the Word of God" was the phrase which became the rallying call of the new movement. It did not mean the revelation of God in history, nor did it mean the inspired Scriptures. It was *sui generis*, but what this in turn meant was not communicable. It was obvious that those who used the phrase were not agreed among themselves, while each was sure that his own interpretation was the *res ipsa*.

A refinement and extension of the new dogmatism came to be known as the "Biblical Theology" in which the ambiguous use of language proceeded apace. By this process a theology of the 20th century is extracted from the historical records of Israel's religion and the early documents of Christianity, but in such wise that history is not the bearer of revelation, and the cultural milieu of this century is no obstacle to accepting a theology based on cosmological, philosophical and theological presuppositions which the civilised world has abandoned.

* *Op. cit.*, p. 69.

We may readily believe that God is the unchanging One, but theology is the human expression and exposition of ideas of God. Only a theology which claims to be almost literally the word of God could accomplish this feat of crossing the ages without variableness of shadow cast by turning. Many seemed to believe that such a theology had now been achieved.

Hence we arrive at a situation in which a historical terminology can be used for the purposes of a dogmatic theology with the advantage that it appears to be of all ages and of none.

A typical instance is the use of the word "event" as a theological conception which nevertheless appears to have historical connotations. Is the "Christ-event" non-historical, a-historical, supra-historical or in no sense an event at all? How then is it known? What connexion has it with the life of Jesus? In what sense is a theology capable of this kind of ambiguity a Biblical theology?

When we come to the particular subject of resurrection and ask whether it is historical, this is regarded as a crude question, almost an insulting one. Yet it is difficult to be sure whether this reaction takes place because one has dared to doubt or one has dared not to doubt the historicity of the resurrection.

When it is said, for example, that "there is no part of the Apostolic Creed which, in our present opinion, expresses the whole genius of the Christian faith more neatly than just that despised phrase, 'I believe in the resurrection of the body'", one can be sure the words do not mean what they say. As it stands the statement could mean that inter-Testamental Jews were Christians before Christ and that the body will rise from the grave, as Ignatius, Jerome and others believed. The probability is, however, that the writer is using traditional language to express some philosophical interpretation of the Christian faith which is quite different from that in the Apostles Creed, and he knows it. Raven's plea for a more exact and accurate use of theological language is in order.

When the early Barth comments on Romans 1:4, "In this declaration and appointment—which are beyond historical definition—lies the true significance of Jesus ... the Resurrection is the revelation, the disclosing of Jesus as the Christ, the appearing of God; the apprehending of God in Jesus" (*Epistle to the Romans*, p. 30), has this a basis in history, although "beyond historical definition", and is the mind of Barth as the mind of Paul in this matter?

Again, when Emil Brunner says that "Easter is not an historical event to be reported" (*Mediator*, p. 573), does he really mean that there never was an Easter, or that it was a supra-historical event; and if the latter, what does this mean?

Where there is no accuracy in the use of language and no attempt to avoid ambiguity, there can be no valid communication between the Christian and the non-Christian, or even between the Christian scholar and the ordinary Christian; therefore no genuine apologetic in modern times. Theology is not religion, nor will it ever fully express religion. But it is useless even as theology if it does not strive to be as unambiguous as possible, as honest as possible. Too often in this period it has been debased by being used as a highly sophisticated means of propagating obscurantism.

In the next chapter we shall notice the attempts which are made to face the modern world in terms which are not dogmatic *à outrance*. The hope of the future is that theologians will learn to speak with scholars belonging to other disciplines on terms of equality and a common pursuit of knowledge. The dogmatic theologian who feels free to insult scientists, philosophers and historians in the confidence that his is the only ear into which God whispers His truth, is a ludicrous anachronism, a 20th-century Simon Magus.

CHAPTER TWENTY-ONE

THE THIN END

AT the beginning of this century Christians in general were convinced of the reasonableness of Christianity. Many were reconciled to the fact that new knowledge would make change inevitable and that possibly some of the things that had been most surely believed would not survive, or at least not in their traditional form. The last thing that seemed likely was a return to dogmatism in any shape.

Yet the most striking fact about the history of theology in this century is precisely the rise of a new dogmatism. From the early thirties a new climate of opinion has been formed, the quest of the historical Jesus abandoned, and the Christian faith presented on a take-it-or-leave-it basis. Neo-orthodoxies of various brands have been propagated with this attitude in common, that the Gospel is essentially a divine encounter in which God bursts in from above and beyond ordinary existence; it needs no apology and can have none. The Word of God comes direct to man perpendicularly if it comes at all. He must simply believe and receive; he has neither the right nor the ability to inquire or ask for reasons why he should believe.

While it would be untrue to suggest that this theology in its most rigorous form had found general acceptance, there can be no doubt that the new dogmatism had the effect of withdrawing Christianity from the conflict of forces in the real world of the 20th century into a smug and self-righteous retreat. It turned the thought of Christians in upon themselves and their faith and substituted a holy introspection for what used to be called the good fight of faith. Psychologically it provided a restoration of confidence, but ethically and intellectually it has been a blight upon Christian thought and action.

If we inquire what effect this has had on thinking about the subject of resurrection, the simple answer is that it has wrought confusion. It has appeared to give new sanction to the traditional creed and encouraged those who are neither convinced Barthians, nor convinced opponents of Barthianism, to think that it is still possible to meet and repulse historical criticism. It has also introduced a new ambiguity into controversy by encouraging apologists to retire to the dogmatic position when they find that they are getting the worst of it in fair argument on the historical issue. It has helped to perpetuate arguments which otherwise would have been abandoned because they are no longer cogent.

The opinion on resurrection which is commonly regarded as orthodox, and is characteristic of all popular religious journalism and preaching today, is that the resurrection of Jesus is a historical event which took place a few days after the crucifixion and that this can be supported by evidence and argument. This is the widespread view of what Christians should and do believe.

This opinion, as indicated above, is generally augmented by the conviction that, even if it cannot be substantiated by historical method, it is nevertheless true and the basis of a theological understanding of resurrection as "a transcendent event". This is the dogmatic complement to the traditional type of argument for the resurrection as historical.

The traditional argument in its simple form is based on

a three-fold appeal to Scripture, the Church and the individual Christian experience. Insofar as this is an appeal to facts of history, it is subject to historical criticism
and to this aspect of the subject we now turn.

The traditional apologist is obsessed by the need to
defend the resurrection of Jesus as event and dogged by
the fear that this may not be possible. These are the
crucial questions: Can the resurrection-narratives in the
New Testament be treated as evidence for a historical
event? Is the existence of the Church an argument for
resurrection as a fact of history? Can the experience of
individual Christians be treated as confirmation of the
occurrence of an incident in past history? It is true that
the traditional attitude regards the resurrection as more
than an event in past history, but is it able to substantiate
the claim that it is at least that?

This form of apologetic is very often liable to be con-
victed of question-begging and a chronic inability to detect non-sequiturs. Because of the introspective climate
noted above, what is offered is too often simply support
to the faith of believers rather than a genuine apologetic.
Very often the traditional apologist seems to think he has
a right to expect his arguments to be treated with kid-
gloves. More often, while professing to set forth a rigorous case which is to be accepted on its merits, he secretly
feels secure in the belief that even if his arguments are
feeble, his case cannot be lost. Faith more than makes up
for the deficiencies of the incompetent advocate.

We must make it clear at this point that it is not being
suggested that theological belief and conviction do not
have their own importance in religious life and experience. What is being objected to is the habit of accepting
a challenge on a historical issue, and then feeling free in
the middle of the argument to break off the contest and

claim victory on the ground that, after all, the issue is not really a historical one.

If we turn to the kind of statement that is usually made of the orthodox position, we do not intend to deal with it in detail but only to illustrate its insuperable weaknesses and ambiguities.

An argument about historical fact, based on the acceptance of the New Testament post-crucifixion narratives, is still very common. But while these narratives are of signal importance, they can no longer be put to this use. One reason for the rise of the new dogmatism was the realisation of this fact.

Even if this were not so, the anomalies in the narratives themselves would make them tools that break in the hands. Nevertheless, the attempt is repeatedly made to do the impossible with the impossible. Thus one apologist says, "The accounts of the appearances of Jesus are difficult to harmonise into a coherent story. The events of the first Easter are difficult to form into a consecutive plan."* This is meretricious mis-statement. Anyone who has tried, knows that it is not difficult: it is impossible.

But the apologist is convinced that his conclusion is sound and therefore his argument must be sound as well. Hence it is propounded that the very unsatisfactory nature of the accounts is testimony to "their truth", which is not the truth of any one of them or of all of them together. This is difficult, but let us admit that it might not be impossible, provided certain conditions are present.

Let us admit that witnesses of the same event often give divergent accounts of what took place. The fallibility of the human mind in this respect is well known. This is the favourite analogy, but is it valid?

In the first place, what is in question here (i.e. in the

* A. M. Ramsay, *The Resurrection of Christ*, Fontana, 1961, p. 48.

matter of resurrection) is whether in fact an event "took place". All the argument so far states is that, *if* the resurrection of Jesus was an event, some degree of diversity in the accounts of it is understandable. But the accounts themselves do not establish that we are dealing with historical event and the degree of diversity, in some instances amounting to direct contradiction, may have quite another explanation.

Again, what we have are not the accounts of eye-witnesses in any case. There is no report from an eye-witness of the resurrection as event in the whole of the New Testament. This means that the degree of diversity is not that between eye-witnesses but something both wider and at a further remove than anything which would allow the use of the proposed analogy in a strict argument.

When one comes across an instance of a well-known writer using this argument from diversity as evidence for resurrection as event, and the same argument as evidence against the Virgin Birth as event, one is reduced to despair of popular apologetics.

Let it be emphasised once more that what is at issue here is the method by which it is attempted to maintain that the resurrection of Jesus can be proved to be in some sense a historical happening. It may be believed to be so, but it cannot be proved by these means to be so.

As to the argument from the existence of the Church, there is certainly substantial historical evidence that the belief that Jesus is Messiah risen from the dead created the Church. But is this to be equated to confirmation of a particular event to be designated the rising of Jesus from the dead? The same kind of obstacles are encountered in passing from the one to the other as we met above.

This is true also of individual Christian experience.

Without questioning the validity of the individual's distinctive Christian experience or the sincerity of Christian belief, it has still to be demonstrated that this can go any distance at all towards affording proof that a specific historical event occurred. The kind of argument it does support is surely of a theological rather than a historical nature.

The failure to establish traditional belief by these means, explains the eagerness with which the neo-orthodox theology was welcomed. Here was a release from a losing battle. Here was a way of securing all at no risk whatever. It was now sufficient simply to announce the tenets of the faith. No more apologies!

But there were those who were fearful of the cost of the new dogmatism. They were aware that the doctrine of resurrection is sterile if it is regarded primarily from the point of view of historical event. But they had a dread of surrendering the historical basis. Was it not possible to comprehend both the old and the new within a theology of mediation or moderation, avoiding the weaknesses of both and drawing on the strengths of both?

The upshot was the rise of an apologetic which avoids the head-on question as to whether the resurrection of Jesus is a historical event in the sense accepted by the traditional apologists, and assumes that the validity of its evangelical exegesis is secure, whether the traditional position is accepted or not.

This is obviously a transitional stage. The apologist cannot find firm footing for a belief in resurrection as event, but knows not where to turn. Shall he abandon the traditional opinion? or reinforce it by a dogmatic theology? or is there some position which no longer requires a historical resurrection and at the same time is not tied to a dogmatic theology?

That sensitive theologian, Canon O. C. Quick, is per-haps the best representative of the apologist in the midst of this unresolved dilemma. He is firmly convinced that history is the sphere of God's redemptive work and at the same time aware that a new kind of Christian apologetic is needed. But it is difficult to say what his answer would have been to the strictly historical question, even if at times he appears to be answering it.

"The New Testament finds the beginning of the new world, the pledge of the final end in the resurrection of Christ. But in the minds of the earliest Christians that belief was inevitably associated with a Jewish cosmology which time has proved to have been partly mistaken and which no one today can altogether accept. How then can the New Testament help towards a really Christian eschatology which retains the essential value of Jewish thought, while discarding its crudities and errors? That perhaps is the most profound and difficult and urgent question which faces Christian theology today. I believe the answer is to be found in a spiritualised doctrine of resurrection founded upon a spiritualised doctrine of sacrifice." *

In this passage the resurrection is "a beginning" and "a pledge". Is it therefore event? It is also a "belief in-evitably associated with an outmoded cosmology". Is it still an event? It is to be "spiritualised". Is this in refer-ence to event or belief or experience?

This appears to be a statement which at some points breaks with the traditional apologetic and puts the em-phasis on the theological implications not of a fact of past history but of a doctrine which is capable of revision.

On the other hand, if we consult his *Doctrines of the Creed*, pp. 146–150, we find the .traditional apologetic.

* *The Gospel of the New World,* p. 111.

Quick argues that the historical critic is not likely to be convinced that the resurrection did happen—unless he is a believer! Clearly he is thinking of resurrection as an event which, he agrees, cannot be historically founded, but which nevertheless is required to be accepted, presumably for dogmatic reasons.

This section is worth detailed study as a classic instance of the insecurity and ambiguity of this position. Quick is never sure whether he is defending the resurrection as event or as doctrine. He moves from one to the other as suits his argument at the time. This is not casuistry: it is a necessity of his presuppositions and he is prepared to put up with it, rather than revise these presuppositions.

Not many are so well aware of the variety of moods and possibilities that exist in theology today. Quick is still anxious to ensure that Christianity is capable of a genuine defence in the modern world. He is not willing to surrender entirely to the new dogmatism, even if he has not been successful in finding a way beyond it.

But in many quarters there is no attempt to reason, only an injunction to accept or reject the dogmatic claims of the neo-orthodox theology. The assumption is that once the act of acceptance is made, there will be no difficulty in holding the traditional conception of resurrection, with or without evidence. Faith is regarded as the instrument for testing as well as receiving the claims of theology. Believe and you will know. But it is not explained how faith can establish whether an event took place. Even belief that Jesus is the Son of God, while it may insure that an event is not impossible, is not equivalent to proving that it in fact took place.

If we take another example of the neo-orthodox position, in this case a "neo-Calvinist", we have a more rigidly authoritarian attitude and a more definite refusal to consider the need for any kind of substantiation as far as the resurrection is concerned. It is definitely event whatever else, but this is not provable.

"We cannot begin to understand how it happened. The Gospels cannot explain the Resurrection; it is the Resurrection which alone explains the Gospels. Here is the mightiest of the mighty acts of God, foreign to the common experience of man, inscrutable to all his science, astounding to believer and unbeliever alike."*

This is remarkably like saying that explanation is both impossible and unnecessary. We note the emphasis on assertion and the absence of exposition, the stress on the unbridgeable gulf between common experience and experience of God, the tilt at man's science, and the devotion to the miraculous. Understandably, Whale did not devote one of his lectures to this mightiest of the mighty acts of God.

The same writer in another connexion is quite capable of seeing how difficult it is to believe on someone else's *ipse dixit*. "Roman theologians are required to teach that the bodily assumption of Mary is true; that it happened as an event in historic time; but they must teach at the same time that no one ever witnessed it. In short, it is dogma rather than history which is here victorious; dogmatic tradition is added to historic truth and preferred to it."†

When is dogmatism not dogmatism? When it is "orthodox"?

* J. S. Whale, *Christian Doctrine*, p. 69.
† J. S. Whale, *The Protestant Tradition*, p. 235.

CHAPTER TWENTY-TWO

VIRTUE AND NECESSITY

In previous chapters we considered three of the 20th-century attitudes to the subject of resurrection. Before proceeding to outline some other attitudes to be found in present day theological writing, it might be as well to recapitulate.

The traditional position, adopted in all popular expositions of the Christian faith, is based on the assumption that Jesus rose from the dead on the third day and that this is a historical event in time and place whose consequences are continuous in the life of the Church. This event can be substantiated by historical evidence such as is to be found in the New Testament documents. It is believed that, in so far as it is historical, it can be shown to be so. The unbiased inquirer can find sufficient evidence to support belief in its historicity.

The neo-dogmatic position is the child of historical scepticism and theological certitude. In its full-grown form it affirms the resurrection as historical event, while scorning the very idea of attempting to support the affirmation by anything so mundane as historical evidence. It would appear that such theological assertion could have nothing to say about what happened in history, but the neo-dogmatist asserts that he knows on divine authority that Christ rose from the dead. This knowledge is inclusive of historical fact, but he has no need of historical evidence.

What may be called the mediating position is really an

uneasy compromise between the other two. It arises from the recognition that the traditionalist is unable to produce the evidence necessary to his case, and that the neo-dogmatist has "solved" the problem by cutting the Gordian knot. He regards the resurrection as at least an event in history. That it cannot be historically vindicated is a misfortune, but when "its" effects are considered, they are sufficient to warrant belief. This attitude appeals to those who are too knowledgeable to accept and too tentative to reject either of the others.

The interesting feature is that in all three cases the relation between history and theology, between Christianity as historical religion and Christianity as religious experience, is the question at issue. The first attitude seeks a historical origin as well as historical confirmation of the things most surely believed. The second is violently anti-historical. The third desires to find some rational synthesis of the historical and the theological which will transcend the felt historical difficulties. Thus, however fashionable it may be to despise historical criticism, it is this despised factor which instigates the reactions of theology in the 20th century.

New movements of thought in recent times have called in the assistance of what are virtually philosophical considerations, though their users would call them religious or theological. For the most part the intention has been to justify or amplify what are essentially dogmatic attitudes to the historical-theological issue. The largely unintentional result has been to make it even more obvious that the traditional position is doomed and to introduce still further confusion on the main issue. The truly historical question is generally avoided and the answer which would be given, if it were pressed, could not be the traditional one and might require to be one of scepticism.

Four quasi-philosophical attitudes are to be considered. They concern ideas of history and time, myth and symbol, existence and, finally, linguistic analysis. We shall briefly indicate these attitudes and their bearing on the subject of resurrection. The literature is extensive.

The attitude of theologians in recent years to the nature of history and the validity of historical method is an interesting example of the exploitation of one discipline by another. The theologian, like the metaphysician, is always tempted to lord it over other seekers after knowledge. This is the natural tendency of their quest for an over-all design in the configuration of existence. It often leads to a premature assumption of success. Numberless tomes of Systematic Theology and Dogmatics are now no more than sad, recurrent monuments to the intellectual arrogance or naïveté of a bygone age. It would have been, and certainly today undoubtedly is, more realistic to accept the evidence that theology has no command over other branches of learning and no way of protecting itself against the impact of new knowledge, short of refusing to recognise its existence.

The theory of history beloved by many theological writers today is characteristically one which has largely been concerted for the chief end of theological exposition. It goes back to Bengel, the Swabian theologian, who maintained that events recorded in the Bible are not simply chronological. They unfold a divine purpose of redemption and must be interpreted in accord with this teleological principle. Bengel's "*heilsgeschichte*" becomes today "the Biblical principle of historical interpretation". Otto A. Piper frankly states that it is used "to overcome the dilemma into which historicism had brought the theologians".

But is this a principle of historical interpretation? The

relation between "*heilsgeschichte*" and history is that between a theory of divine activity and the meaning of the course of human existence. Tillich, Brunner, the early Barth, and Bultmann, for example, have little interest in history, even that recorded in the Bible, except as it can be seen to symbolise Gospel truth. But writers such as Cullmann, Piper, C. H. Dodd, A. Richardson, claim that history can be truly interpreted only through some such conception as "*heilsgeschichte*". The purpose of God as seen in the Bible is the "organising centre of all history". It will take up or "gradually transform" all history into itself.

The attitude to the untheological or "mere" historian is generally supercilious. He does not possess the key to historical interpretation. If he is presumptuous enough to ask whether some of the things the theologian regards as history are history, he is promptly accused of trying to disprove Christianity.[*]

If he wants to write on Christian origins, let him first become a Christian, otherwise he will infallibly misinterpret the facts, if not fail to see them altogether. This attitude is capable of an interesting psychological explanation.

This theological principle makes an assertion of duality in history; historian's history is overlayed by or otherwise related to the theologian's conception of the ultimate meaning of existence, which we might call theologian's "history". Theoretically, this allows that the resurrection may belong to the latter while remaining unperceived or unperceivable as history. Thus the resurrection is "seen to be history only by the eye of faith" (Barth), or is "a transcendent occurrence" (Brunner, C. H. Dodd). There are, however, serious objections to the theologian's

[*] Cf. A. Richardson, *Christian Apologetics*, p. 89 ff.

appropriation of the word history to an alien use and it is relevant to inquire how anything called history or occurrence could be perceived only by the eye of faith. This, of course, is no denial of the existence of faith or the validity of the concept of transcendence; nor is it a denial that history is not to be equated with incident simpliciter.

Is "the Biblical principle of historical interpretation" really Biblical? There is a considerable difference between the Biblical belief that God is the Lord of history and the theory that the only true principle whereby history may be interpreted is to be derived from the Bible. The former can and does exist apart from the latter, and there is no guarantee that only one theory of this kind could be excogitated from the Scriptures. Does belief in God implicitly convey a theory of the interpretation of history? The Bible may be able to provide one (it is not itself one) only on hermeneutic principles which have a dogmatic basis. It requires to be read in before it can be read out. Even so, it is surely a theological conviction rather than a principle of historical interpretation.

Sometimes the resurrection is spoken of as if it did not belong to theologian's "history" with a possibly undetectable historical aspect, but as if it were a unique point of intersection between these two, and that its "reality" is established by postulating this unique characterisation. Interesting and, in some ways, fruitful as this conception may be, it is still susceptible to the question whether it has any validity and what kind of "reality" it attributes to the resurrection. Theologically, it certainly departs from the traditional conception of revelation as centred on the life, teaching and death of Jesus, events amenable to historical interpretation.

The new principle of interpretation only appears to

afford an interpretation of history, but history is not really its province; its subject matter is not event but faith. It can properly tell us nothing of resurrection as event, i.e. whether it is an event and if so what is its nature. It may have much to tell us of resurrection as a tenet of faith, but it is designed to evade rather than to solve the historical problem.

The interest in the relation between "Symbolism and Belief", to quote the title of Edwyn Bevan's famous series of Gifford Lectures, has produced some of the most original thinking of recent times. It is impossible in this context to do more than indicate the kind of problem which the examination of the meaning of myth and symbol tries to solve and what light it throws on our own subject.

Religious myths are generally regarded as the projection of religious faith. They "foster and interpret" man's relation with God in terms and language appropriate to the time. They themselves, because of this temporal element, must be reinterpreted if they are to continue to be a valid representation of spiritual truth. Have they any necessary connexion with historical event and what justification is there for regarding some of the Christian doctrines as mythological?

There are some doctrines that are truly apprehended as representations in story form of something that is true of human nature. "Eden is on no map . . . The Fall refers to a dimension of human experience which is always present."*

It is held by some that symbol, image and metaphor convey truth which cannot be conveyed in a conceptual form. Much argument has arisen on whether this is true for always or only for the time within which the basic

* J. S. Whale, *Christian Doctrine*, p. 52.

presuppositions of the age in which the myth arose still hold good.*

It is admitted that the Fall is not history. What are the bounds of such a mythological explanation and interpretation of truth which was once accepted as literal and historical? Obviously the crucifixion is not in this category, while (for many) the ascension and (for some) the virgin birth are. What of the resurrection? Bultmann regards it as something known not as history but by faith, as a symbol of the saving power of Christ's death. Whether it is anything more than this he does not precisely say. "To every other eye than the eye of faith, the action of God is hidden."

Tillich also regards the Cross and the resurrection as together meaning one thing. For him they represent Jesus as the Christ of God. But for him they are both historical. "In both cases something happened within history. Otherwise the Christ would not have entered history and could not have conquered it."† As far as the mode of conceiving the event of resurrection is concerned, he asserts that neither "body" nor "appearance" are adequate categories, but "it has the character of spiritual presence" and yet is not mere subjective experience.

It is doubtful whether this approach has led us any further, however fruitful otherwise, e.g. as an exposition of the meaning of belief in the resurrection of Christ for Christians today. It is not made clear in what sense historical event is regarded as being capable of mythological significance, e.g. the Exodus, the crucifixion. Nor is it clear that truth conveyed mythologically without known counterpart in history is capable of being validated except to faith. The fact seems to be that mythological truth is

---

* Cf. the de-mythologization controversy in *Kerygma and Myth*, etc.

† *Systematic Theology*, Vol. II, p. 177.

truth of experience and not necessarily truthfulness of historical event and it cannot refer backwards in confirmation of anything that can be said to have happened.

The emphasis on experience rather than history, on the Christian life rather than on the traditional creedal content of the Christian faith, is seen to best advantage in those theologies which make use of an existential philosophy and introduce the principle that "a personal interest must lead and define the hermeneutic questions of the scholar" (Erich Dinkler). Again it is admitted that this approach is aimed at overcoming historicism, dependence on the reconstruction of the past, by stress on the present nature and future destiny of man.

Berdyaev stated as follows the philosophical viewpoint of those who find in existentialism a new and worthwhile mode of interpreting Christianity to the present age: "If we are to look at the relation between truth and revelation philosophically, it can only be done by a philosophy which is inwardly based upon religious and spiritual experience, not by a rationalist philosophy but by an existentialist philosophy which recognises that spiritual experience is primary." *

The movement traces its ancestry to Sören Kierkegaard and, in Bultmann for instance, makes much of Heidegger's distinction between "authentic" and "unauthentic" being. Dr. John Macquarrie has provided a good introduction to the subject in his book *An Existentialist Theology* (S.C.M. Press).

We are not concerned with the argument as to whether it is legitimate to interpret the Christian faith in terms of an external philosophy, or with the general problems that arise from such a proceeding. The resulting theology appears to cut the link between historical event and

* *Truth and Revelation*, p. 8.

present existence by making the content of the Christian creed refer almost completely to the here and now and the open future. Neither the resurrection nor the Cross can be known to us as happenings in history but only as they confront us with a present challenge to our actual existence.

Existentialists adopt one of two attitudes to the historical question regarding the resurrection. Either they are content to state that the historical question is unimportant, without answering whether in their belief "a resurrection" took place, or they assert the resurrection as historical event while denying that it can be substantiated as such. In both instances this is simply avoidance of the issue. While behind the theology of "the Cross" lies the actual crucifixion, it is left problematical as to whether behind the theology of "the resurrection" there is anything that can be called a historical rising from the dead. Thus Bultmann equates faith in the resurrection with faith in the saving efficacy of the Cross.* At least to the extent that the Cross is related to the crucifixion, the Christian faith appears to be historically founded. But faith in the saving efficacy of the Cross is not directly equivalent to belief that Jesus died on the Cross, so that the historical connexion still remains undefined and certainly unprovable on these terms. It is "the word of preaching" that confronts us as the word of God. We must not ask for credentials. History has no evidential value for faith.

While the service of the existentialists to the understanding of experience is not in question, it can hardly be said that their handling of the historical problem has registered any advance except to cut off any retreat to the traditional view.

Recently some attention has been given to the use of

* *Kerygma and Myth*, p. 41.

language in religion and to whether religious language is always symbolic and distinct from the factual language of science. This inquiry merges with that into the relation between mythological statements of religious truth on the one hand and knowable historic events on the other.

We have seen the difficulties that arise in the latter investigation and the same kinds of dilemma are present when the attempt is made to state in specific instances whether the language used is religious language referring to religious truth or whether there is at the same time or quite separately a reference to historical event. Once again the difficulties are pronounced in reference to the resurrection.

In his book *Religious Language*, Dr. Ian T. Ramsey alludes to the subject in such a way as to suggest that the Christian's references to the resurrection are in religious language and not the language of history and science. But this is followed by the inevitable qualification.

On page 127 he says that the question "Did the resurrection occur?" has *not* the same logic as "Did the empty tomb occur?" if for no other reason than that "the second can be asserted while the first is denied, and the second might even be, and by some has been, denied while the first has been asserted".

This appears to be an unequivocal statement to the effect that when the Christian confesses his faith in the resurrection, he is saying nothing about whether he is referring to a historical event. Indeed, he may be persuaded that there is no evidence for such a historical event and therefore no reason for any assertion that such an event "took place". Nevertheless, because he is a Christian he believes that such an event did take place, if we may judge from the tenor of the remark that it is "important to ask the right sort of questions about the

Resurrection, and especially important not even to start discussing questions which imply that the Resurrection is what it could not be if the Christian claims for it were true" (p. 131). In other words, an assumption must be made which it is not Christian to question.

But if the point at issue is whether "the Christian claims for the Resurrection are true", this phrase, in the above context, appears to be simply a form of words whereby the point is avoided. What answer would be given to the question whether the Christian as Christian ever makes statements about history? Does the Christian's understanding of history have no effect on the nature and colour of his beliefs as a Christian?

If Dr. Ramsey is saying that a religious person is religiously affected by a religious relation to a religious context which, in this case is designated "belief in the Resurrection", no one will dispute it. It tells a good deal about "a religious person". But what else?

In summing up it seems only reasonable to conclude that what we have witnessed in recent years is the breaking of the traditional ties between the efficacy of belief in resurrection as a Christian experience on the one hand, and an event in history called the rising of Jesus from the dead after crucifixion on the other. Whether in the future these sundering bonds can be strengthened is clearly very doubtful. In any case the idea of resurrection is consciously being used as a means of interpreting existence; in the first instance the existence of Jesus and then of those who believe in Him.

EPILOGUE

THE MIRROR OF FAITH

THE MIRROR OF FAITH

I N the preceding chapters we have looked at the subject of resurrection from various angles but our purpose has been severely limited. The idea of resurrection is one which is capable of enveloping human thought within its uncharted depths.

All who are fascinated by the mind of man sooner or later come face to face with this mystery: it is capable of the resurrection concept. Modern science, psychology and philosophy are not engaging their full possibilities till they come to grips with it. This may be the significance of quotations like the following:

"I can see no reason why death, in the nature of things, need be inevitable."*

"For every piece of conscious life that loses its importance in value—so runs the law—there arises a compensation in the unconscious."†

"The radical defect in all forms of belief in progress, as they are expressed in positivist credos, is that they do not definitely eliminate death. What is the use of detecting a focus of any sort in the van of evolution if that focus can and must one day disintegrate?"‡

"The greatest truths are those which stand on the dizzy verge of the inconceivable and yield to the soul fore-shadowings of a stupendous enigma."§

* William S. Beck, *Modern Science and the Nature of Life*, p. 286.
† C. G. Jung, *Modern Man in Search of a Soul*, p. 241.
‡ Teilhard de Chardin, *The Phenomenon of Man*, p. 270.
§ Keyserling, *Immortality*, p. 6.

But such vast and perilous expeditions are not our subject and are mentioned only to ensure that there is no mistake about the very circumscribed area within which we have been working. What is intended in bringing this book to a close is to re-emphasise three facts which tend to be overlooked in discussions of the subject.

The first is simply that the subject has a history. If this were remembered it would cut short many thoughtless and extravagant statements on the part of Christian apologists. Christians did not discover the idea of resurrection. It did not burst on the world as a new and splendid concept in the middle of the 1st century A.D. It was already fully developed before the 1st century opened. Nothing new was added by Christian writers to the conception itself as distinct from the context in which it was held.

It may be objected that to the Jew resurrection was simply a matter of hope, whereas to the Christian it is a matter of fact. This, however, is not so. The only persons to whom it could conceivably have been a matter of fact are those who could have testified that they saw Christ arising from the dead. To all other Christians it is not and cannot be a matter of fact. Briefly we may say that to the Jew resurrection was a matter of hope, to the Christian a matter of faith and hope, but to neither a matter of fact.

If this should seem to be a serious disadvantage to Christian apologetics and Christian theology, that is very regrettable; but this may be so simply because we tend to ask we know not what, requiring only history where what is possible is faith, refusing value to a concept because it is not a stone or an action, forgetting that the human spirit is spirit.

The second point is that it is in association with Jesus

that the idea of resurrection created Christianity. This is different from and additional to saying that Christianity began as an apocalyptic religion or that, as R. H. Charles rightly says, "It was from the apocalyptic side of Judaism that Christianity was born." It is to say that the distinctiveness of Christianity owes its reality to the distinctiveness of Jesus and the thought of His followers concerning Him.

This also has its bearing on Christian apologetics. What is at the heart of the Christian faith is not doctrine but a person capable of creating or inspiring Christian doctrine. The centrality of Jesus ought not to be negated by ethical, theological, mystical or eschatological propositions. They do not create Him but He creates them. The Person of Christ is and remains the crux of Christianity.

It follows that the truth of Christianity is not in propositions but in inspiration, not in the logic of doctrine but in the life of personal relation. When we talk of Christian doctrine we are talking theology. This has its necessary place. But theology is not religion. How far astray we can go in this direction is indicated by the fact that the Apostles' Creed neglects to mention that God is love and we ought to love one another.

That Jesus is the only person of whom it could be believed that He rose from the dead in any sense which is not synonymous with magic is the fact that created the Christian faith. If Christianity should perish it will be through neglect of that fact, for which no amount of learned theology will compensate.

Finally, the doctrine of resurrection is a doctrine. It is not a deduction from fact but the creation of faith. The inter-Testamental history makes this quite clear. Faith is a creative force in its own right, one of the noblest attributes of the human spirit. It does not create out of fact, only at the instigation of fact.

This raises the question of the relation between faith and truth. But that which is creative does not wait upon logic. If faith waited to be confirmed by knowledge it would no longer be faith. And however disquieting it may be to our neat systems of epistemology, what faith creates can not be uncreated because it is uncomprehended within the terms of our logical processes. A quack may effect a cure which all his quackery cannot be arraigned to gainsay. Belief even in an illusion (looked at from outside the believing context) is not itself illusory nor are its effects.

Perhaps the bounds we set in our minds to both faith and truth disqualify us from ever discovering their ultimate relation. Meantime we have no better guide than that by their fruits we shall know them, even if this does mean the denial of any immediate possibility of knowing, since the fruits do not appear till after the event.

Faith created the doctrine of resurrection; it comes to fruition in Christianity; and the only belief in a future life which is anything to the purpose is that which is itself the creation of faith.

To express it in unsophisticated terms, if I have eternal life I ought to feel it in my soul—it ought to be the life I now live in the flesh by faith in the Son of God. This is how it signifies its existence; this is how it bridges any gulf that exists between the "now" and the "not yet". Or again, as living souls we live by faith and faith is that by which we relate ourselves to the unknown present and the illimitable future.

All expressions of certainty regarding the future are falsified if they are regarded as doctrinal certainties and not as certainties of conviction.

Insofar as Christian theology has not taken the trouble to make this distinction clear to the believer, it has condemned him in some matters to the agony of confessing with his mouth what his heart does not believe, while at the same time he bears in his heart what he has no adequate means of confessing.

It is sometimes argued that this is a necessary state of affairs since we are dealing with the imponderable. But there is a difference between imponderable and incredible. To many who regard "and the life everlasting" as imponderable but not incredible, "the resurrection of the body" is both ponderable and incredible.

This kind of ambiguity could be responsible for alienating from the organised Church an increasing number of devout men and women who have no other religious allegiance.

It is true that the Church has a large and noble function in society and good pragmatic reasons may be given for Church membership. But can the Church afford to run the risk of recruiting its members on a pragmatic basis only? Must it not continue to grapple with the problems of truth and the mysteries of existence?

If the Church takes the risk of refusing to face intellectual difficulties for the sake of mass appeal, miscalled evangelism, it is liable to become like a hospital service which has no medical research department. The concern to spread the Gospel by making new converts must include inspiring the most thoughtful members of the community to confess and exemplify the Christian faith in the changing world of today.

BIBLIOGRAPHY

Baillie, J., *And the Life Everlasting* (O.U.P.); *Our Knowledge of God* (O.U.P.); *The Belief in Progress* (O.U.P.).

Barth, K., *Romans* (Hodder & Stoughton); *Credo* (Hodder & Stoughton).

Beck, W. S., *Modern Science and the Nature of Life* (Pelican).

Berdyaev, N., *Truth and Revelation* (Centenary Press); *The Destiny of Man* (Centenary Press).

Bethune-Baker, J. F., *An Introduction to the Early History of Christian Doctrine* (Methuen).

Bettenson, H., *The Early Christian Fathers* (Oxford).

Bevan, E., *The Hope of a World to Come* (Allen & Unwin); *Jerusalem under the High Priests* (Arnold); *Symbolism and Belief* (Fontana).

Bornkamm, G., *Jesus of Nazareth* (Allen & Unwin).

Brinton, C., *The Shaping of the Modern Mind* (Mentor).

Brunner, E., *The Mediator* (Lutterworth); *Man in Revolt* (Lutterworth).

Bultmann, R., *Jesus and the Word* (Fontana); *Primitive Christianity* (Thames & Hudson); *The Theology of the New Testament* (S.C.M.).

Cadbury, H., *The Peril of Modernising Jesus* (S.P.C.K.).

Charles, R. H., *Religious Development between The Old and New Testaments* (Clarendon).

Collingwood, R. G., *The Idea of History* (Oxford).

Cross, F. M. Jr., "The Dead Sea Scrolls", art. in *The Interpreter's Bible*, Vol. 12 (Abingdon).

de Burgh, W. G., *The Legacy of the Ancient World* (Macdonald & Evans).

de Chardin, T., *The Phenomenon of Man* (Collins).

Dibelius, M., *A Fresh Approach to the New Testament and Early Christian Literature* (Ivor, Nicholson & Watson).

Dodd, C. H., *The Apostolic Preaching and its Developments* (Hodder & Stoughton); *The Parables of the Kingdom* (Nisbet); *History and the Gospel* (Nisbet).

Glasson, T. F., *The Second Advent* (Epworth).

Grant, F. C., Mark (exegesis) in *The Interpreter's Bible*, Vol. 7 (Abingdon); *Ancient Judaism and the New Testament* (Oliver & Boyd).

Grant, R. M., *The Letter and the Spirit* (S.P.C.K.).

Guignebert, C., *The Jewish World in the Time of Jesus* (Routledge & Kegan Paul).

Hanson, Leaney & Posen, *A Guide to the Scrolls* (S.C.M.).

Harnack, A., *What is Christianity?* (Williams & Norgate).

Huizinga, J., *The Waning of the Middle Ages* (Pelican).

Jackson & Lake, *The Beginnings of Christianity*, Vol. 1 (Macmillan & Co.).

James, E. O., *The Social Function of Religion* (Hodder & Stoughton); *The Beginnings of Religion* (Hutchinson).

Josephus, *The Jewish War*; *The Antiquities of the Jews*.

Jung, C. G., *Modern Man in Search of a Soul* (Routledge & Kegan Paul).

Keyserling, H., *Immortality* (Oxford).

Kiddle, M., *Revelation* (Hodder & Stoughton).

Klausner, J., *Jesus of Nazareth* (Allen & Unwin).

Lake, K., *The Historical Evidence for the Resurrection of Jesus Christ* (Williams & Norgate).

Lewis, H. D., *Freedom and History* (Allen & Unwin).

Lietzmann, H., *A History of the Early Church* (Lutterworth).

Loisy, A., *The Birth of the Christian Religion* (Allen & Unwin).

Macgregor & Morton, *The Structure of the Fourth Gospel* (Oliver & Boyd).

Macquarrie, J., *An Existentialist Theology* (S.C.M.).

Manson, T. W., *The Teaching of Jesus* (Cambridge).

Manson, W., *Jesus the Messiah* (Hodder & Stoughton).

McLeman, J., *The Birth of the Christian Faith* (Oliver & Boyd).

Montefiore, C. G., *The Synoptic Gospels* (Macmillan).

Niebuhr, R., *The Nature and Destiny of Man* (Nisbet).

Oesterley & Robinson, *History of Israel* (Oxford); *Hebrew Religion* (S.P.C.K.).

Pfeiffer, R. H., *History of New Testament Times* (Harper).

Quick, O. C., *The Gospel of the New World* (Nisbet); *Doctrines of the Creed* (Nisbet).

Ramsey, A. M., *The Resurrection of Christ* (Fontana).

Ramsey, I. T., *Religious Language* (S.C.M.).

Raven, C. E., *Good News of God* (Hodder & Stoughton); *Science, Religion and the Future* (Cambridge).

Richardson, A., *Christian Apologetics* (S.C.M.).

Robinson, H. W., *Religious Ideas of the Old Testament* (Duckworth); *The Christian Doctrine of Man* (T. & T. Clark).

Robinson, J. A. T., *Jesus and His Coming* (S.C.M.).

Russell, D. S., *Between the Testaments* (S.C.M.).

Schoeps, H. J., *Paul: The Theology of the Apostle in the Light of Jewish Religious History* (Lutterworth).

Schweitzer, A., *The Quest of the Historical Jesus* (A. & C. Black); *The Mysticism of Paul the Apostle* (A. & C. Black).

Scott, C. A., *Christianity According to St. Paul* (Cambridge).

Scott, E. F., *Revelation* (S.C.M.).

Tillich, P., *Systematic Theology* (Nisbet).

Toynbee, A., *A Study of History*, Vol. VI (Oxford).

Various Authors, *Kerygma and Myth* (S.P.C.K.).

Wake, W. C., "The Pauline Corpus", *Journal of the Royal Statistical Society*, Series A, Vol. 120.

Webb, C. C. J., *A History of Philosophy* (H.U.L.).

Werner, M., *The Formation of Christian Dogma* (A. & C. Black).

Whale, J. S., *Christian Doctrine* (Fontana); *The Protestant Tradition* (Cambridge).

Widgery, A. G., *Interpretations of History* (Allen & Unwin).

INDEX